Gospel Poverty

Essays in Biblical Theology

Gospel poverty

Essays in Biblical Theology

by

Augustin George S.M.
Jacques Dupont O.S.B.
Simon Legasse O.F.M.
Philip Seidensticker O.F.M.
Beda Rigaux O.F.M.

Preface
by

Constantine Koser O.F.M., Minister General

Translated
and with a Preface
by

Michael D. Guinan O.F.M.

FRANCISCAN HERALD PRESS
1434 WEST 51st STREET • CHICAGO, 60609

Gospel Poverty, Essays in Biblical Theology edited and translated by Michael D. Guinan, O.F.M. from the French *La Pauvrete Evangelique*, Les Editions de Cerf, 1971, Copyright © 1977 by Franciscan Herald Press, 1434 West 51st Street, Chicago, Illinois 60609.

Library of Congress Cataloging in Publication Data
Main entry under title:

Gospel poverty.

Translation of La Pauvrete evangelique.
Papers presented at a symposium on poverty held in Rome, June 23/25, 1970.
Includes bibliographical references.
1. Poverty (Virtue)—Biblical teaching—Addresses, essays, lectures. I. George, Augustin.
BS680.P47P3813   241'.6'99   76-44548
ISBN 0-8199-0610-7

NIHIL OBSTAT:
Mark P. Hegener O.F.M.
Censor Deputatus

IMPRIMATUR:
Msgr. Richard A. Rosemeyer, J.C.D.
Vicar General, Archdiocese of Chicago

January 12, 1977

MADE IN THE UNITED STATES OF AMERICA

Preface

The message of gospel poverty, set by Christ as leaven in the heart of humanity, upsets and disturbs the Church of today. Vatican Council II was well aware of it, recalling in its quest for purification and renewal that Jesus Christ "for your sake, made himself poor though he was rich" (2 Cor 8:9) and that "the Church, although it needs human resources to carry out its mission, is not set up to seek earthly glory, but to proclaim, even by its own example, humility and self-sacrifice." The Council adds: "The Church encompasses with love all those afflicted by human infirmity and recognizes in those who are poor and who suffer, the image of its poor and suffering founder. It does all it can to relieve their need and in them it strives to serve Christ" (*Lumen Gentium*, 8).

During these past ten years, critical reflection in the Church has continued to progress while the contrast between what Christ has called us to and the concrete human condition becomes more vitally apparent. Studies, research, attempts at renewal, and various other tensions upset a false security and pro-

voke a strong current of return to "the purity of
gospel life." Within this movement, the Franciscan
Order experiences an acute need for an examination
of conscience and a return to the sources of its ideal
of poverty.

The first thing to be done, it seemed to us, in order
to arrive at an accurate idea of Christ's demands and
at a precise vision of the way in which they can be
lived in the actual condition of the world and of the
Church, was to search the Sacred Scriptures, seeking
to reach as much as possible the call of Jesus himself. Every society must seek within its origins the
light and élan for its renovation.

To this end we sought out professors of Sacred
Scripture who have been especially interested in the
theme of gospel poverty. Despite the inevitable com-
plexity of the problems involved, we asked them to
present to us as exactly as they could what biblical
study on this question has to say today. Fr. Beda
Rigaux O.F.M., professor at the University of Louvain, graciously accepted our invitation to organize a
meeting of top-level exegetes and to plan with them
a symposium on poverty. This meeting was held at
Rome, June 23-25, 1970. The following participated:
Augustin George S.M., professor on the Catholic Faculty of Lyons; Jacques Dupont O.S.B., monk of St.
André, Belgium; Simon Légasse O.F.M. Cap., professor on the Catholic Faculty of Toulouse; and Philip
Seidensticker O.F.M., professor on the Faculty of
Theology at Paderborn. Fr. Rigaux was prevented from
attending at the last minute, but was able to send the
text of his study.

The presentations of these specialists enable us to
view the *status questionis* for the Old Testament, the
evangelists, and St. Paul. The high quality of the
papers seems to us to make their publication very de-
sirable, so that they might reach a wider audience.

They do not, of course, present us with a picture complete in all its details. The authors themselves raised this objection. (Scruples of the masters!) They did recognize, however, how useful it would be to place these works at the disposition of those who might wish to pursue further research in this area.

We believe these pages will be a precious help for those who seek to orient themselves seriously on the road of gospel poverty. We also believe that in this present moment of this Church, such a work as this, of reflection and analysis, might provide some excellent guidelines for the study of other pressing problems, for example, the ministry, the pursuit of peace, justice, morality, and revealed truth.

We strongly hope that this collection will bring clarity and will help in finding, among so many equivocations and utopian dreams, the road of authentic gospel poverty .

FR. CONSTANTINE KOSER O.F.M.
Minister General

Santa Maria Mediatrice
Rome, Italy

TRanslator's Preface

While the problem of riches and poverty is hardly new in the life of the Church, today it is posed for us in an especially acute way. Pressing social problems within the United States, as well as our relationship to other countries in the world, make it imperative for us to reexamine not only our collective and individual lifestyles but also the whole question of an authentic Christian response to these problems. The question can be posed briefly: What can gospel poverty mean for the Christian in the world of today?

Both of these terms, gospel and poverty, need elucidation. Poverty is notoriously difficult to define, which should not be a surprise since it is a purely relative term, existing in a real way on a variety of levels. In a political sense, poverty is the lack of power or ability to influence the political processes. At another level, one can be psychologically or spiritually poor in the sense of lacking psychic, emotional, or spiritual resources for coping with problems of everyday living.

Most often, poverty is viewed in its economic sense: the lack of money or material possessions. Socio-economic situations vary considerably from place to place and from time to time, and when we get beyond the minimum level of starving to death, what is "poor" in one ghetto may be relative comfort in another. In the ancient world, the basic distinction was between those who worked for their living and those who did not; we can hear echoes of this in the old moral discussion of "servile" and "liberal" work. While it may offend our American egalitarian sense, I suspect this distinction is not completely irrelevant today.

The word gospel is not as self-evident as it might appear either. We speak of "the four gospels," the "gospel at Mass," the "gospel message," etc. There is, essentially, only one gospel, Jesus Christ; in him the Father reveals and accomplishes the good news of our salvation. In the New Testament we have four versions of the one gospel, the gospel *according* to Matthew, Mark, Luke, and John. The rest of the New Testament witnesses to this one gospel too, as does the Old Testament in preparing for Christ. To "live the gospel" means to live an authentic Christian life—to incarnate, as it were, Christ in our lives and in our world. The experience of the Church through the ages also plays a role in our efforts to understand and live the gospel, and within this experience the Scriptures play a central role. Vatican II, in its decree on divine revelation, continually repeats the need of the Church to root her life and renewal in a profound grasp of the Scriptures: "Like the Christian religion itself, all Church proclamation must feed on, and be ruled by, holy Scripture" (21).

As we seek an authentic gospel poverty, then, the teaching of the Scriptures—all of them—plays an essential part. But what kind of guidance can we hope to find there? The Scriptures do not give us a new law code, nor a list of do's and don'ts. We cannot expect detailed answers to our moral questions; circumstances and cultures change too much and too fast for that. Broadly speaking, we can expect to find two kinds of guidelines: negative and positive. Negatively, Christ's teaching may rule out certain kinds of behavior as incompatible with life in the kingdom. Positively, we are presented with goals and ideals, general directions which authentic Christian life must always keep in focus. Jesus' teaching on love, for example, as difficult as it may be in practice, can never be reconciled with hatred of others, even a "holy hatred" of God's "enemies."

In 1970, as part of the *resourcement* of the Franciscan Order, the five essays in this book were delivered at a symposium in Rome. They present some of the finest research currently available relative to the study of poverty in the Bible. While the authors by no means agree on all points of interpretation, a consensus emerges which provides both positive and negative norms to help us as we face our modern problems.

On the negative side, we learn that poverty, in the sense of economic deprivation, of lacking the necessities of life, is never a Christian virtue. The existence of such a situation is a scandal and an insult to the justice of God (A. George). J. Dupont concludes each section of his study with the refrain, "There is no gospel ideal of poverty." If economic poverty were to be a Christian ideal, then so would blindness, lameness, deafness, leprosy, etc., for these are all listed together as evils which the Messiah, at his coming, will alleviate (Lk 4:17-21, 7:22; Isa 60:1-2). The good news to the poor is precisely that their misery is at an end. The only way we can make "poverty" a Christian virtue is to spiritualize it, and this is exactly what Matthew does (5:3).

This teaching, which is clearly in the texts, is often
neglected; it is therefore something we need to focus
on today. It is hard to escape the impression that
some promoters of social reform, from a variety of
positions, lose sight of this and fall into a kind of
romanticization of the poor and their condition. Material
things, they suggest, cannot but corrupt the purity
and integrity of their owners; anyone with possessions
becomes an oppressing enemy. Such a distrust of matter and material things is hardly a new phenomenon
in the Church, as Gnosticism, Manichaeism, and
Jansenism remind us. The gospel corrective to mis-
use of things is not non-use but proper use.

The positive teaching of the New Testament points
to two distinct but interrelated areas. The first is
radical faith in God. Developing out of the Old
Testament spirituality of the ʿănāwim, the "poor in
spirit" of the New Testament recognize their dependence
on God and place their whole lives in his care.
Material things (one's own family is also mentioned)
present the strongest and most common distraction from
this kind of faith. Christians must be ready to sacrifice their possessions if and when they present an
obstacle to their growth in faith. This is the basic
teaching in the gospel story of the call of the rich
man (S. Légasse) and of the "catechism of discipleship" in Luke 14:25-35.

The second area of positive concern is communal
sharing. Jesus preached to the poor the good news
that their poverty was ended. The Christian communities continue his work in their caring for each other
and sharing what they have, so that no one need suffer basic need. It is not that everyone has the same
things but that all are ready to help those who are
less fortunate by sharing what they have (J. Dupont).
In the parable of the last judgment (Mt 25:31-46),
Christ the Judge does not say "I was hungry, but you

did not become hungry with me; thirsty, but you did not become thirsty with me, etc."; he said "I was hungry and you gave me no food." The Christian is called to continue Christ's work of putting an end to the scandalous condition of poverty.

Our modern world desperately needs the living example of authentic gospel poverty that all Christians are called to. The history of the Church, as well as contemporary experience, teaches us how easy it is, without a firm grasp of the whole gospel, to stray into "blind alleys, posturing and rhetoric. . . . What would poverty be then but a harsh and inhumane rigorism, or a social ideology?"[1] These essays can help those in the Franciscan family, for whom poverty, while being neither central nor distinctive,[2] has always been important, avoid these "blind alleys." They can help all religious orders as they seriously examine their lives of vowed poverty in the modern world. They can help all Christians ask and face certain basic questions about riches, poverty, and the Christian life. For these reasons, I thought these essays deserved to be translated and made available to a wider, English-speaking audience.

Several articles provide extended discussion in footnotes of rather technical points and bibliographical references to a great many French and German works. Since the reader who is interested and able to use these works would have access to the French original of this work, I have at times modified and condensed footnote material. Whenever I have done this, I have ended the footnote in question with an asterick(*). The last article, by Fr. Rigaux, was enriched with sixty-nine footnotes of very useful and extensive reference material. In consultation with the publisher, I have omitted almost all of these for the reason given above, retaining only a few general notes. The New American Bible has been used for the biblical texts. Quotations were made from the Paulist Press: *De Ecclesia: The Constitution on the Church of Vatican Council ii;* the Liturgical Press: A. Gelin, *The Poor of Yahweh;* and the Franciscan Hearld Press: B. Rigaux, *The Letters of St. Paul: Modern Studies.*

In preparing this translation, I owe thanks to many people but would single out especially Pierre Etchelecu O.F.M., my "native control"; Kenan Osborne O.F.M., my "friendly Dean ", who would ask frequently—but never innocently—"Aren't you done yet?" and John Keating S.J., who used this book for a course on Luke-Acts and first brought it to my attention.

MICHAEL D. GUINAN O.F.M.

Franciscan School of Theology
Berkeley, Calif. 94709

Footnotes

1. D. Flood and T. Matura, *The Birth of a Movement: A Study of the First Rule of St. Francis* (Chicago: Franciscan Hearld Press, 1975), pp. 124, 128. The quotation is by Fr. Matura.

2. T. Matura, in *Birth of a Movement*, pp. 123-124.

Contents

Abbreviations

DBS	Dictionnaire de la Bible, supplement
EB	Estudios biblicos
HUCA	Hebrew Union College Annual
IDB	Interpreter's Dictionary of the Bible
JBC	Jerome Biblical Commentary
NRT	Nouvelle revue theologique
NT	Novum Testamentum
NTD	Das Neue Testament deutsch
NTS	New Testament Studies
PG	Patrologia greca (J. P. Migne)
RB	Revue biblique
RGG	Die Religion in Geschichte und Gegenwart
RHPR	Revue d'histoire et de philosophie religieuses
VT	Vetus Testamentum
TDNT	Theological Dictionary of the New Testament (G. Kittel)
ZKT	Zeitschrift für katholische Theologie
ZNTW	Zeitschrift für die neutestamentliche Wissenschaft und die Kunde der älteren Kirche

The Scriptures
and Religious Poverty

Poverty in the Old Testament

Augustin George S.M.

If we wish to arrive at an understanding of Jesus' thinking about poverty, we must begin by examining what poverty meant for the Old Testament, since this is where Jesus found both his vocabulary and the point of departure for his thought. The vocabulary and ideas of the Old Testament on poverty, however, are quite different from our own, the former arising from a totally different mentality and sociological context.[1] Here we set ourselves the task of seeking to describe the Old Testament meaning of poverty.

To avoid any ambiguity, let us be precise: we understand the word poverty in its modern sense, "the state of a person who lacks material resources, money; insufficiency of resources."[2] In order to proceed correctly in our research, it would also be helpful to

present certain preliminary data dealing with (1) the
vocabulary of the poor in the Old Testament and (2)
the sociological context of poverty in Israel.

I. Preliminary Data

A. Vocabulary of the Poor in the Hebrew Old Testament

In keeping with its customary, concrete approach to
things, the Old Testament speaks less of poverty and
more often of the poor. These latter are mentioned
some 245 times by six main terms (ʿānî, ʿānāw, ʾebyôn,
dal, rāš, and miskēn)[3], all of which our modern trans-
lations render, more or less frequently, by "poor."[4]

We can treat ʿānî and ʿānāw together because both
derive from the same Semitic root and because they
were in fact often confused by ancient scribes (it is
difficult to distinguish them, for example, in the
manuscripts from Qumran). The basic meaning of the
root is still under discussion;[5] for most, it refers to
"the action of bending or stooping" or to "the state
of being bent over." A. Rahlfs makes it even more
precise: "to take the attitude of a servant before his
master"; H. Birkeland proposes "to be weak, small,
thin", and from this it comes to mean "to have less
strength or worth"; E. Bammel prefers "to be in a
situation of having to respond or answer." At any
rate, the root describes a situation of social inferiority.
This corresponds well to the usage of the terms which
the texts often apply to the oppressed. However, over
the course of the formation of the Masoretic text these
two terms seem to have undergone a semantic evolution in which they became more and more differentiated
from each other.[6]

ʿānî appears 80 times: 70 in the law codes, 25 in
the prophets, 32 in the psalms, 16 in the wisdom
writings. It is a verbal adjective of passive form,
designating "one who is stooped over, who gives

in, who submits." The Septuagint (LXX) translated it by *ptōchos* (38 times), *penēs* or *penichros* (13 times), *tapeinos* (9 times), and *präus* (4 times). The various translators of the Bible of Jerusalem translate it, according to the context, by "poor", "destitute", unhappy", "afflicted", "humble", etc.

'anāw is used 25 times and always in the plural (*'anāwîm*), except in Nb 12:3, a fact which seems to indicate a tendency to apply it to a group. It appears in Nb 12:3, in the prophetic writings of the eight and seventh centuries (7 times), in the psalms (13 times), and in the wisdom writings (4 times). It refers, at times, not only to the humbled and oppressed but also to the humble and the gentle (but was the primitive text *'anî* or *'anāw?*). Thus the LXX translates it by *präus* (8 times), *tapeinos* (6 times), *penēs* (4 times), and *ptōchos* (4 times), while the Bible of Jerusalem renders it 5 times by "poor," 2 times by "unhappy," and 15 times by "humble." It is very likely that, as time went on, the moral and religious meaning of the term was stressed, especially by the Masoretes.

The word *ebyôn* appears 61 times in the Hebrew bible: 9 times in the law codes, once in Esther (9:22), 17 times in the prophets, 24 times in the psalms, 10 times in the wisdom writings.[7] It must come from a root *'ābâ* ("to wish, desire"). Concluding his study on the use of this term in the Old Testament, P. Humbert observes that "if it is appropriately applied to the poor . . . , it implies a further key idea, that of begging. At one and the same time, the *ebyôn* is a poor person and a beggar" (p. 6). The LXX renders it by *penēs* (29 times), *ptōchos* (10 times), *adunatos* (4 times), and *tapeinos* (twice); the Bible of Jerusalem translates it most often by "poor," but several times by "indigent," "unfortunate," "humble," etc.

Dal is used 48 times in the Hebrew text: 5 times in the historical books, 4 in the law codes, 13 in the prophets, 6 in the psalms, 20 in the wisdom writings. The root *dalal* means "to be weak, feeble, puny," and the texts use it to designate the weak in both a physical and a social sense. The LXX translates it by *ptōchos* (23 times), *penēs* or *penichros* (10 times), *asthenēs* or *asthenein* (5 times), *adunatos* (3 times); the Bible of Jerusalem translates it by "poor," "feeble," "destitute", "pitiful."

Rash appears 21 times: 4 times in the books of Samuel, once in Ps 82:3, 14 times in Proverbs, and twice in Qoheleth. It is a participle of the verb *rûsh*, which means "to be deprived, needy." The LXX translates it by *ptōchos* (9 times), *penēs* (6 times), *tapeinos* (once), and the Bible of Jerusalem by "poor," "needy," "begger."

Misken appears four times in Qoheleth and twice in the *Hebrew* of Ben Sira (Ecclesiasticus 4:3 and 30:14). This rather rare term is used in Assyria and at El Amarna and seems originally to indicate "one who is dependent, submissive. The LXX translates it by *penēs* in Qoheleth and by *prosdeomenos* and *ptōchos* in Ben Sira; the Bible of Jeruslaem by "poor," "needy," "indigent."

This vocabulary expresses an understanding of poverty quite different from our own. For our modern languages, as already in Greek and Latin,[8] poverty is the lack of goods; it is an economic idea. While Hebrew sometimes considers poverty a lack (*rāsh*) or a situation of begging (*ebyôn*), it views it primarily as a situation of dependence (*'ani, 'anāw, miskēn*) or weakness (*dal*). In the biblical mind, the poor person is less one who is indigent and more one who is oppressed, an inferior or a lesser one. It is a social idea. This is why later, when the poor begin to spiritualize their condition, their ideal will not become detachment from the goods of this world but rather a voluntary and loving submission to the will of God.

B. Biblical Poverty in Its Sociological Context

From the time of Moses and down through the New Testament period, Israel always knew the poor, the small and humble; and shifting political situations and social structures profoundly marked its thinking on this topic.[9]

While it is difficult for us to form a precise picture of Israel at the time of Moses, we can affirm that it was a time of collective poverty in the economic sense of the term. But it was also the time when the least social differentiation existed among the people; everything was held in common, from their poor goods and possessions all the way up to their national destiny. This deep solidarity would always remain one of the aspects of the "desert ideal" (Ps 68:8-11; cf. Dt 15:4).

The settlement in Canaan and the sedentarization of the people brought the division of the land among the tribes, clans, and families, and from the point of departure for a differentation of social conditions. Although the old accounts of the books of Judges and Samuel and the archeological excavations at the tenth-century level[10] show that this differentiation was rather moderate, social problems already begin to appear. The oldest sections of the Covenant Code are preoccupied with the protection of slaves (Ex 21:1-11, 20-21, 26-27), and the laws of Ex 22:20-23:11 are probably almost as ancient.[11] These are much concerned with the resident alien (the *ger*; Ex 22:20, 23:9, 12), the widow and the orphan (22:21), the *'anî* who borrows (22:24), the *dal* and the *ebyôn* who have lawsuits (23:3, 6), and the *ebyôn* in the sabbatical year (23:11).

The eighth century opened a period of particularly serious social crisis. The prophets of that time set themselves violently against the luxury of the great ones, both in Israel (Am 3:12, 15, 4:1, 5:11, 6:4-7;

Hos 7:5, 8:14. 10:1, 12:9; Isa 9:9, 28:1) and in Judah (Isa 2:7, 13-16, 3:16-24, 5:8-12, 32:13-14), and against the crushing yoke with which they were weighing down the poor (cf. below). Archeology confirms these data, showing a characteristic distinction between the rich quarters and the poor quarters in the city from this time on.[12] This crisis seems to have had its origin in the progress of urbanization, in the development of relations with foreign powers, and in the extension of the royal administration, which greatly multiplied high-level functionaries, etc.

At the end of the eighth century the intervention of Assyria suppressed the kingdom of Israel (in 721) and crushed that of Judah, first under the labor of defense (Isa 22:8-11) and then under tribute (2 Kgs 16:8, 18:14-16). This improverishment of the kingdom affected everyone, especially the poorest. Deuteronomy, published in 621 during the reign of Josiah, shows a singular concern for the poor, including the Levites, whom the reform had deprived of their local sanctuaries (cf. Dt 14:29, 16:11, 14, 26:12-13, 27:19). Then came the victory of Babylon in 605 and the deportation of Jehoiachin in 597-598, along with the notables of Jerusalem (2 Kgs 24:14-16). Only the poor people remained (the *dal*; Kgs 24:14), and part of these too were deported, in 587-586 (2 Kgs 25:11-12).

The return from exile in 537 begins a period of austerity. For those who had left the rich lands and prosperous businesses of Babylon, life in Judea was harsh (Hg 1:6-9; Zec 8:10). They had the difficult task of rebuilding a modest temple (Hg 2:3; Ezr 3:12), while their Samaritan neighbors opposed their work of reconstruction (Ezr 4; Neh 3:23-4:2). The poor Jews suffered from famine and had to sell their children into slavery to obtain food to live and to pay the king's tax (Neh 5:1-5).

Because of the lack of historical works from this

time, we are poorly informed about the social situation of the Persian and Greek periods. It is clear, however, that the long political peace and the fertility of the land were conducive to general prosperity.[13] We find several indications of this in the third-century papyrus of Zeno,[14] and in the first century in the buildings and general extravagance of Herod the Great. But royal luxury brings with it crushing taxes,[15] and, in a more general way, the enrichment of the "haves" renders the condition of the "have nots" much more painful. And the have nots were very numerous indeed at the time of Jesus, as both the gospels and the Jewish texts indicate.[16]

II. The Meaning of Poverty

In Israel's life, then, poverty was a constant and painful fact, manifesting itself especially in its consequences: dependence, humiliation, and oppression. We must now study what Israel thought of this poverty.

The Old Testament texts on this subject cover a wide range of differing evaluations which we can classify systematically under four headings:

A. Appreciation of profane wisdom
B. Religious judgment on poverty: It is a punishment
C. Religious judgment on poverty: It is a scandal, a breach of covenant
D. Different approaches to the religious acceptance of poverty

We will examine each of these different points of view in order, but we must be on guard against any simplistic systematization. We are always tempted to view the Old Testament as a uniform progression, reaching its fulfillment in the gospels. The fact of the matter is that the four approaches to poverty we have just listed coexisted, not only throughout the Old Testament period but they can still be found among people of today.

A. *Appreciation of Profane Wisdom*

Israel's wisdom writings, which willingly pick up the thought of older, pagan wisdom, often give us the judgments of human wisdom on poverty. It is attributed to laziness (Pr 6:6-11, 10:4, 20:4, 13, 24:30-34), to idle talk (Pr 14:23), to idle pursuits (Pr 28:19; cf. 12:11), to the seeking of pleasure (Pr 21:17, 23:20-21; Sir 18:32-19:2). What we see here are observations based on everyday human experience, which could be verified even today. Their value consists in exhorting us to work and to take life seriously.

But these observations do not apply to every case, nor do they resolve all the problems presented by riches and poverty. Israel sensed this from its very beginnings, and so always sought to view poverty in relation to the justice and grace of its God.

B. *Religious Judgment on Poverty: It Is a Punishment*

The first reaction of the religious person of antiquity in the face of poverty was to interpret it within the schema of temporal retribution: poverty is an evil, therefore it is a punishment. This evaluation, appearing in all the ancient religions, can be found throughout the history of Israel.

This goes hand in hand with the view, also found through the Old Testament, which regards riches as a divine blessing. The ancient stories recount with admiration the prosperity of God's friends. In Genesis it becomes almost a refrain in the history of the patriarches. "Now Abraham was very rich in livestock, silver and gold" (Gen 13:2; cf. 24:35); Isaac "became richer and richer all the time, until he was very wealthy indeed. He acquired such flocks and herds, and many servants" (Gen 26:13-14); Jacob "grew

increasingly prosperous and he came to own not only
large flocks but also male and female servants and
camels and asses" (Gen 30:43; cf. 32:6, 33:11).

The books of Kings enthusiastically detail the riches
of Solomon (1 Kgs 10:14-25): they are a gift of God
(1 Kgs 3:13; cf. Sir 47:18). The law codes conclude
with blessings which promise temporal prosperity of every
kind to all who observe the law of the Lord (Dt
28:3-12; Lv 26:3-10). The sages vie with one another
in proclaiming the riches which God grants to the just
(Pr 10:22, 15:6, 19:23, 28:25; Sir 11:21-25, 31:8-11).
It is a dogma for Job's friends (Jb 5:17-27, 22:28)
and the lesson that is added later to the same book
(Jb 42:10-12). The wisdom psalms too take up the
classic teaching (Ps 1:1-3, 37:25, 112:1-3).

Within this perspective it is not surprising that
poverty was seen as a divine sanction for some fault
or failure. It is one of the curses which those who
transgress the law codes are threatened with (Dt 28:15-
46; Lv 26:14-26); the prophets address the same
curse to sinners (Isa 3:16-24, 4:1, 5:9-10); and those
who are oppressed wish the same upon their adversaries (Ps 109:10-12). The wisdom writings formulate
this opinion as a statement of doctrine (Pr 13:18, 21,
25; see especially Job's friends, noted above: Jb 5:1-7,
15:26-35, 20:22, 27:13-23).

These views contain some valid elements: a sense of
the values of this world, for example, or—especially—
a deep faith in the justice of God. Their weakness
lies in considering the justice of God only within the
tight framework of temporal retribution. They were
without the knowledge of the transcendent destiny
which God grants to his own.

It is to the credit of both pagan and biblical
wisdom that they felt the insufficiency of this solution
and realized that, in some way, poverty was also a
scandal.

C. The Scandal of Poverty

Despite this classical theory of retribution, it is very surprising that the sages, first pagan and then Israelite, saw poverty rather often as something abnormal. This is surely because the observation of experience quickly showed that the poor person is not always a sinner nor is the rich person always just (cf. Mi 6:12; Jb 21:7-12; Ps 73:1-14; Pr 16:8, 19, 19:1, 22, 28:6; Sir 13:17-20). It is precisely because poverty appeared as something abnormal that a believer, standing before God, sought to relieve it: (1) those who surrounded the poor person, by charitable assistance, and (2) the poor person by recourse to God in prayer.

1. The *duty of giving assistance to the poor, the widow, and the orphan* appears from most ancient times—in Mesopotamia and Egypt as well.[17] Above all, it is the duty of the king; he, above all, has both the sovereign initiative and power. Many texts show that the poor, the feeble, and widows and orphans were especially protected favorites of the king.[18]

In Israel, even before the rise of the monarchy, the obligation of helping the poor is formulated in the Covenant Code.[19] This deals with the defense of the slave (Ex 21:1-11, 21, 26-27), the widow and orphan (22:20-23), the *'ānî* who borrows (22:24), the *ébyôn* with a lawsuit or during the sabbatical year (23:6, 11). While these commandments were inspired by earlier Middle Eastern legislation and wisdom, the Mosaic covenant gave them a new meaning, the inferior condition of the poor and the humble was felt to be a breach in the solidarity and unity of the people of God. And the covenant Lord has a special concern for the "disinherited" members of his people.

Within this perspective of the covenant, the prophets of the eighth century undertook the defense of the poor, who were the victims of the social crises of their time. They denounced all forms of oppression which economic development was bringing in its wake: tribute and crushing rent (Am 4:1, 5:11-12; Isa 3:14-15), fraudulent business dealings (Am 8:4-6), the monopolizing of land (Mi 2:1-3), the selling of penniless debtors into slavery (Am 2:6, 8:6), unjust legal sentences (Am 5:12; Isa 10:1-2, 32:7; Jer 5:28, 22:16), and all forms of violence (Ez 16:49, 18:12-13; Zec 7:10). To counteract this, Isaiah introduced into his portrait of the Messiah-King the old royal ideology of the king as protector of the poor (Isa 11:4). A century later Jeremiah, in order to condemn the abuses of Jehoiakim, showed this ideal realized in Josiah, his father (Jer 22:15-16).[20]

Under the influence of the first prophets, the Code of Deuteronomy further developed the prescriptions of the Covenant Code in favor of the poor. This is particularly clear in the laws on the tithe (14:29, 26:12-13), the sabbatical year (15:1-11), the slave (15:12-18), feasts (16:11, 14), and the protection of weak people (24:10-21, 27:19). A. Causse has drawn attention to the "charitable tendencies" of this legislation and connects them, correctly, with a concern to restore the ideal community of the people of God.[21]

The same concern for the poor can be found in the Holiness Code (Lv 19:9-10, 13, 23:22) and in the Psalms (41:2, 82:3-4, 109:16, 112:9). In the wisdom writings, the exhortation to help the poor appears frequently, both in the style of older wisdom (Pr 21:13, 31:20 (the traditional theme of the king as protector of the poor appears in Pr 29:14 and 31:8-9)) and with an explicit religious motivation (Pr 14:21, 31, 17:5, 19:17, 22:9, 22-23, 28:27, 29:7; Jb 29:12-16, 30:24-25; 31:16-23; Sir 3:30-4:10, 7:32-36, 29:8-13).

In the most recent books of the Old Testament, the help given to the poor receives the technical name *sedaqa*, "justice," the accomplishing of the will of God (the Septuagint will translate this by *eleemosyne*, from

which, through the Latin, our word "alms" derives):
Sir 3:30, 7:10, 12:3, 17:22, 29:8, 12, 31:11, 40:17,
24; Dn 4:24; Tb 2:14, 4:7-11, 16, 12:8-10, 14:2, 8.[22]

Among Israel's predecessors, both in Mesopotamia and
in Egypt, the protection of the poor appears first to
have been a royal function, before becoming a function of the gods. In Israel, the movement seems to
have been just the opposite. The instiution of the monarchy came after the establishment of the covenant
and is thought to have developed out of it.[23]

2. Face to face with the scandal of poverty, the poor
person expected help from those in his community, but,
above all, *he addressed himself to God in prayer.* The
prayers of the poor are numerous in the Old Testament—that of the humble Hannah (1 Sm 1:9-20), for
example—but it is especially in the Psalter that the
greatest number of these prayers are gathered together.
The question of just who these "poor" are has often
been discussed, and often they are said to be "the
spiritually poor."[24] While the nature of the psalms as
prayer naturally moved the poor to "spiritualize" their
condition (we will return to this below), it is also
clear that the psalms of the poor were, for the most
part, composed by the unfortunate, the humbled, the
oppressed; and the "spiritualization" of the texts seems
especially to be the work of those who reused them in
a private or liturgical "re-reading."

In these texts, the "poor" cry out for help from
God (Ps 10:12, 25:16, 40:18, 69:30, 70:6, 72:2, 74:19-
21, 86:1, 88:16, 109:22—in all these texts the word
'*anî* is used). They proclaim their hope in divine intervention, whether they call themselves *èbyôn* (Ps 9:19,
12:6) or '*anî* (Ps 9:13, 14:6, 18:28, 35:10, 140:13) or
'*anāw* (Ps 10:17, 22:27, 25:9, 37:11, 76:10).

Often these prayers of the poor conclude with a
thanksgiving which affirms that their request has been
heard, as in Jer 20:13, where the prophet describes

himself as an *ĕbyôn*. Sometimes we are dealing with an *ĕbyôn* (Ps 107:41, 109:31; cf. at Qumran, 1 QH 2:32, 5:14, 16, 18), at other times with an *'ānî* (Ps 22:25, 68:11; cf. Qumran, 1 QH 2:34, 5:13), or an *'ānāw* (Ps 34:3, 7, 69:33-34, 147:6, 149:4), or a *dal* (Ps 113:7, 1 Sm 2:8), or a *rāsh* (1 QH 5:20).

This prayer is based solidly on the traditional belief in the God who protects the poor (Ex 22:20, 26: Dt 10:18; Pr 15:25; Sir 21:5, 35:12-22). The psalmist often affirms it explicitly (Ps 10:17; Ps Sol 5:2, 7, 10, 15:2, 18:3). The prophetic promises of the salvation of the poor support it (Isa 11:4, 19:20-22, 29:19, 41:17, 49:13, 61:1, 25:4, 26:6; cf. Ps 37:11, 72:2-4, 12-13); the sages say quite freely that God "will do justice for the poor" (Jb 5:8-16, 36:6-15; Sir 11:12-22, 35:11-24). But we are not dealing with the egalitarian justice of Greco-Roman law. Here it is the justice of the covenant, the justice of the grace of the Lord, who saves the poor because he loves them.

D. *Different Approaches to the Religious Acceptance of Poverty*

This is a delicate subject. While the "spiritual poverty" of the *'ānāwîm* is often discussed, the expression is rather equivocal. If we understand the expression to mean that the poor of the Old Testament arrived at a mystique of renouncing temporal goods, we must admit that this kind of detachment simply does not exist in the Old Testament. This is the new contribution of Jesus. Until he came, poverty, in any meaning of the term, was considered an evil: we must fight against it by communal assistance; we ask God unceasingly to deliver us from it; at best, we can consider it a test to educate us (Ps Sol 16: 13-14); we always hope to be saved from it, and this salvation was conceived only in terms of this world, with its temporal values.

The painful experience of poverty, however, often led the poor to accept their present condition with trust in the God who loves the disinherited and will save them. In this sense, we can speak of a "spiritual poverty" in the Old Testament, a submission to the mysterious will of God (cf. Job), an acceptance of the condition of being "small" because God loves the poor. This is not yet evangelical poverty, with its devaluation of terrestrial goods and its radical detachment. But it points in that direction.

Since we recognize in Jesus the goal of God's revelation, we can look back in the Old Testament and discern several paths which led the people of God in the direction of evangelical poverty.[25] They are:

1. Criticism of riches
2. Religious understanding of humility
3. Outline of a choice between God and mammon

1. *Criticism of Riches*. We noticed above that the Old Testament often sees in riches a divine blessing, a sign of being a friend of God. Experience, however, quickly taught the faithful how inadequate this opinion was. Simple human wisdom had always been able to recognize that riches are very fragile indeed (Pr 28:22; Qo 5:13; cf. Lk 12:33, 16:9); that they bring anxiety and worry with them (Qo 5:11; Sir 31:1-2); that they are worth less than honor (Pr 22:1) or health (Sir 30:14-16). Nor can the wealthy take' their riches with them to the tomb (Ps 49; Qo 5:14, 6:2-3; Sir 14:4, 15; cf. Lk 12:16-21).

But Yahweh's faithful ones noticed especially that riches are often tied to injustice. Although the prophets do not expressly identify them as such, the oppressors of the poor, whom they attack, are apparently the rich. (The identification between "the rich" and "the wicked" appears only in Isa 53:9; Enoch 46:7, 94:8-10,

96:4, 97:7-10).[26] The wise, above all, sought to analyze how riches lead to sin: they denounce riches as the source of pride (Pr 28:11), of not believing in God (Pr 30:9), and, more precisely, of rooting one's faith in earthly goods, which turns one away from trust in God (Ps 52:9; Pr 11:28; Jb 31:24; Sir 5:1-8, 11:18-19; Enoch 94:8).

These experiences and opinions did not conclude by condemning being rich nor by refusing riches, but they relativized their value and moderated their use (Pr 30:7-9; Qo 5:17-19; Sir 29:23). We see here a wisdom which, while perhaps a little shortsighted, is already a prudence which faith can clarify and a proper warning against greed.

2. *Religious Understanding of Humility.* The traditional faith in Yahweh as the protector of the poor gradually brought about a new consideration of poverty. While it is always an evil, it also gives one a special title to the favor of God. This perspective led the poor to accept their condition and to give it some meaning. We can speak, then, of a spiritual poverty which is a submission in faith, an accepted smallness, a religious humility. This deepening of persepctive can be attributed to the prophets.[27]

Isaiah directed all his efforts against pride—the source, in his opinion, of the lack of faith of the governing circles of Judah (Isa 2:6-22, 3:9, 15, 29:14, 30:1) and of Ephraim (9:8-9, 28:1). He demands total abandonment into the hands of God (2:22, 7:9, 8:6, 28:16, 30:15-18) and promises salvation to the poor (11:4, 14:30-32, 29:19-20). He does this because, for him, salvation consists only in complete trust in God and humble submission to his mysterious plan.

Zephaniah is the only prophet to demand, in parallelism with justice, *'ănāwâ,* the humble submission to the will of God (2:3). Before Ben Sira, the word is found only in Pr 15:33 and 22:4, both of which connect it

with fear of the Lord, and in Pr 18:12, which makes
it the condition for honor. Zephaniah proclaims that
on the day of salvation, the remnant of Israel will
be "a people humble and lowly (ʿānî wādal) who will
take refuge in the name of the Lord" in opposition
to the "proud braggarts", whom God will have pushed
completely aside (3:11-13). A hope of this kind is far
from the political and military dreams which so often
weighed down royal, messianic expectation. Zephaniah
has drawn his lesson from the history of Judah, humili-
ated by Assyria; he had understood that God grants
his salvation to those who accept his will. Humility
is for him the source of justice and retains its value
even when the time of salvation shall have come.

Jeremiah, persecuted and saved, praises the Lord
"because he has rescued the life of the poor (ʾebyôn)
from the power of the wicked" (20:13; at Qumran,
this passage inspired 1 QH 2:32, 5:18). He was not
someone who was particularly indigent, as we can sur-
mise from 32:6-15, but he was persecuted and, as
such, can invoke the benevolence of God for the victims of injustice. Indirectly, then, he proclaims that
his weakness was the source of his salvation.

The psalmists are not at all removed from this way
of thinking when they present themselves as poor. Their
distress is certainly real enough; they are sick, humili-
ated, attacked, oppressed. But they accept their unfortunate condition until the time that it should please
the Lord to remove them from it. They see in this
condition a title to the divine favor. In naming themselves "the poor," they think of themselves as "the
privileged of the Lord" and proclaim their humble
trust in his benevolence.

Those who re-used these psalms after their composition were not always in the same painful situation of
their original authors. It was especially this group that
tended to "spiritualize" the poverty of the psalms. But

to the extent that they entered into the faith and humility which inspired the psalms, they did not falsify the original prayer.[28]

One or two centuries before Jesus, the priests at Qumran defined themselves readily as *ĕbyônîm* (1 QM 11:9, 13; 1 Qp Hab 12:3, 6, 10) or "the community of the *ĕbyônîm*" (1 QH 5:22; 4 Qp Ps 37 1:10, 2:10). By this they did not intend to indicate they had renounced money, despite the fact that they held their goods in common; they expressed, rather their persecuted condition (1 Qp Hab 12; 1 QH 2:32-34, 3:25, 5:13-22) and their ideal of humble submission to God in faith (note the insistence on *'ănāwâ* in their rule: 1 QH 2:24, 3:8.8, 4:3, 5:3, 25, 9:22, 11:1).[29]

In this way the experience of concrete, material, and especially social poverty seems to have led the people of the Old Testament to submit themselves humbly into the hands of God and to trust in his grace. It is, strictly speaking, not an idealization of poverty, since this was never for them a value in itself. But poverty *did* have an indisputable religious richness for them: it called them to open themselves to God and prepared them to receive both the demands and the gifts of Jesus.

3. *Outline of a Choice between God and Mammon.* In examining these approaches to a religious understanding of poverty we have up to now followed only negative paths: the discovery of the insufficiency of wealth and the renunciation of human sufficiency by humility. What remains to be done is to follow a more positive route, leading to the poverty of Jesus: the discovery that God is the sole value.

It is not necessary to spend much time in showing that God was the supreme value for Israel from its very beginning. His word, his cult, his law always come before anything else. And if he is a demanding Lord, he is also passionately loved. He is the Good *par excellence,* preferred for his own sake without discussion, to all others. Ps 16, 36:6-10, 42:2-3, 63:2, and 84:2-6, for example, express attitudes which can easily be found in the oldest oracles of the prophets. This search for God will find its definitive expression in the demands of Jesus and will give meaning to his own radical renunciation.

The Old Testament never expressly posed the choice between God and temporal values because it was not until the time of Daniel that it came to any idea of retribution outside of time. Until then there was always the danger of confusing the search for God and the search for his gifts. It would not be fair or just to accuse the people of the Old Testament of seeking only sordid self-interest. The disinterestedness with which the prophets risked their lives for the mission, without hope of an afterlife (think, for example, of Jeremiah), and the burning love of the psalmists for their God are beyond question. Nevertheless, we do not regularly find in the Old Testament the explicit invitation to renounce all the goods of this world for the service of God. This will be the novelty of Jesus.

Certain exceptional passages, however, are oriented in this direction. The sages many times proclaim the primacy of the fear of God over the goods of this world (Pr 15:16, 16:8). It is not yet a choice between God and mammon because the sages still hope that the justice of God will finally grant them material goods too. But it is already the principle of making generous choices in our everyday lives. The burning exlamations of the psalmists manifest a more ardent tone, as well as a love without doubt more disinterested (e.g., Ps 37:16-17, 73:25-28, 84:11). Even taking into consideration the exuberance of lyric poetry, we cannot help but see that faithful of the Old Testament held more closely to God than to his gifts. Is this not the clearest distinctive approach to the detachment of Jesus?

Conclusion

We have found in the Old Testament a keen sense of the suffering which poverty brings and different strong reactions to this evil. Human wisdom sees in it the consequences of laziness or disorder; faith see in it, each in turn, a divine punishment, a scandal, a call to discover certain religious values.

These different points of view co-exist throughout the Old Testament. They continue to exist today among many Christians. This should not surprise us. Throughout the ages, poverty is one of the forms of the mystery of evil. It is not the kind of intellectual problem which can be solved in theory, once and for all, but a mysterious reality which each one must face in faith, an experience in which each one is personally engaged before God.

Biblical revelation, however, brings a new light to this mystery. It is fulfilled only in Jesus, the fullest manifestation of God and his love. Over a long period of time, the Old Testament groped painfully to prepare for it. Because its vision was restricted to re-tribution within a purely temporal perspective, it was at a disadvantage in its approach to poverty. It lacked the revelation in Jesus Christ of the gift of God and the transcendent destiny of humanity which are neces-sary to orient God's children properly when they are faced with the values of this world. Now that we know Jesus Christ, we can discern in the Old Testament how God was leading his people to the gospel under-standing of poverty.

Footnotes

1. Studies on poverty in the Old Testament abound. We have cited the main ones (up to 1959) in our article "Pauvre", *DBS* 7 (1962) 405-406. Here we would add the following general studies: E. Kutsch, "Armenpflege," *RGG* 1:617-619, "Armut," *RGG* 1:622-623; P. Grelot, "La pauvreté dans l'-Ecriture sainte," *Christus* 31 (1961) 307-322 (collected in *De la Mort a la Vie Eternelle* (*Lectio Divina* 67) (Paris: Ed. du Cerf, 1971), pp. 223-246); L. Roy, "Poor," *Dictionary of Biblical Theology*, ed. X. Leon-Dufour (rev. ed.; New York: Seabury Press, 1973), pp 436-438; W. Grundmann, "*tapeinos*," *TDNT* 8:1-26; R. Leivestad, "Tapeinos, tapeinopron," *NT* 8 (1966) 36-47; J. M. Liano, "Los pobres en el A.T.," *EB* 25 (1966) 117-168; A. Hamman, *Vie liturgique et vie sociale* (Paris-Tournai: Desclée, 1968), pp. 11-27; J. Dupont, *Les béatitudes* (Paris: J. Gabalda, 1969, 2:19-90.

2. This is the definition of P. Robert in *Dictionnaire alphabétique et analogique de la langue francaise* (Paris: Societé du nouveau Littré, 1966) 5:60. He defines the poor person (p. 59) as "one who lacks what is necessary or has only the strictly necessary."

3. See our article in *DBS* 7:387-388 and Dupont, *Béatitudes,* 2:24-34.

4. The Septuagint (LXX) translates the different Hebrew terms in a variety of ways: *ptōchos* (88 times; etymologically, "one who crouches"; in classical usage "a beggar"); *penēs* (67 times; etymologically, "one who works hard"; in classical usage "one who has only necessities and lives from his work by saving"); *tapeinos* (21 times; "one who is low"); *praus* (12 times; "meek"). See our article in *DBS* 7:388-389 and Dupont, *Beatitudes,* 2:20-24.

5. See P. Van den Berghe, "Ani et anaw dans les Psaumes," in *Le Psautier*, ed. R. de Langhe (Louvain: Publications universitaires, 1962) p. 291 (62); Dupont, *Beatitudes,* 2:25.

6. E. Bammel, "*Ptōchos*," *TDNT* 6:892-893; Van den Berghe, "Ani," p. 293.

7. On this word see P. Humbert, "Le mot biblique ebyon,"

RHPR 32 (1952) 1-6. This is collected in *Opuscules d'un hebraisant* (Neuchatel: Secrétariat de L'Université, 1958) pp. 187-192.

8. Dupont, *Béatitudes*, 2:19-24.

9. On the sociological aspects of Israel's history see A. Causse, *Du groupe ethnique à la communauté religieuse* (Paris: Alcan, 1937); S. W. Baron, *A Social and Religious History of the Jews* (New York: Columbia University Press, 1952) vol. 1; R. de Vaux, *Ancient Israel* (New York: McGraw-Hill, 1961).

10. See de Vaux, *Ancient Israel*, pp. 72-73.

11. Some have proposed a late date for this section of the Code (e.g., J. Morgenstern, *HUCA* 33 (1962) 59-105, who considers it added to the Code before 485). Examination of the form of the text and the parallels in older pagan legislation has convinced many authors that a much earlier date is appropriate. See I Lewy, "Dating of the Covenant Code Sections on Humaneness and Righteousness," *VT* 7 (1957) 322-326 (Davidic period), J.L'Hour, "L'alliance de Sichem," *RB* 69 (1962) 361-368 (before the monarchy), etc."

12. De Vaux, *Ancient Israel*, pp. 72-73; P. E. Bonnard, "Poterie," *DBS* 8 (1967) 201-207.

13. See the data on agriculture and commerce in Baron, *History*, 1:250-285.

14. L. Pirot, "Gerza," *DBS* 3 (1938) 627-630.

15. Flavius Josephus reports this in his *Antiquities* (*A.J.* XVI, 5:4, 7:1). See also Baron, *History*, 1:236, 284.

16. Extrabiblical data on this point have been collected by J. Jeremias in *Jerusalem in the Time of Jesus* (Philadelphia: Fortress Press, 1969) 87-119.

17. A. Barucq, *Le Livre des Proverbs* (Paris: J. Gabalda, 1964), pp. 33-34.

18. Dupont has assembled a dossier of texts from Mesopotamia, Ugarit, and Egypt on this point; see his *Béatitudes*, 2:54-65.

19. See fn. 11 above.

20. This ideal is found in Ps 72:2, 4, 12-13 (the date is quite disputed) and also at Qumran (1 QSb 5:21-22), but not in Ps 101 or Ps Sol 17.

21. In *Du groupe ethnique,* pp. 160-177.

22. R. Bultmann ("Eleēmosunē," *TDNT* 2 (1935) 486, fn. 4) notes that "it is difficult to distinguish (in the text of the LXX) between general benevolence and almsgiving." He opts for the latter in Sir 29:8 and Tb 4:7, 16.

23. Dupont (*Béatitudes,* 2:65-66) presents a discussion on this point.

24. On these disputes see my article in *DBS* (7:392) and Van den Berghe, "Ani."

25. This point of view has been studied particularly in the article of Grelot, cited in fn. 1 above.

26. See Bammel, *TDNT* 6:324.

27. A. Gelin has noted the influence of Zephaniah in *The Poor of Yahweh* (Collegeville, Minn.: Liturgical Press, 1964), pp. 29-31, and that of Jeremiah in *Jérémie* (Paris: Ed. du Cerf, 1952), pp. 115-117.

28. It is common today to understand the term *ʿănāwîm* in a spiritualized sense. As we noted above in studying the vocabulary, this seems to be correct in many instances, but we cannot be sure that this spiritualization is primitive. Besides, there are many cases where the word *ʾebyôn* has the same "spiritual" value (e.g., Ps 69:34, 132:15, 140:13 and the Qumran texts, of which we shall speak shortly).

29. See *DBS* 7:394-395; S. Légasse, "Les pauvres en esprit et les 'volontaires' de Qumran," *NTS* 8 (1962) 336-345; J. Dupont, "Les ptochoi to pneumati de Mt 5:3 et les 'nwy rwh de Qumran," in *Neutestamentliche Aufsätze* (Regensburg: F. Pustet, 1963), pp. 53-64; J. A. Fitzmyer, "Jewish Christianity in Acts in the Light of the Qumran Scrolls," *Essays on the Semitic Background of the New Testament* (Missoula, Mont.: Scholars Press, 1974), pp. 271-303 (originally published in *Studies in Luke-Acts: Essays Presented in Honor of Paul Schubert,* (ed. L. E. Keck and J. L Martyn (London: SPCK, 1966), pp. 233-257).

The Poor and Poverty in the Gospels and Acts

Jacques Dupont O.S.B.

The gospels and the Acts of the Apostles do not contain any explicit discussion of poverty. They do, however, devote a fair amount of attention to the poor, meaning especially by this the needy whom we have an obligation to help by our almsgiving. We will begin our study with this first aspect of poverty: it imposes itself on Christians as a demand of charity. Then, in relation to this, we will discuss the practice of sharing material things, the "community of goods," which, according to Acts, characterized the early Church in Jerusalem. In a third part we return to the gospels. Here the poor are presented in some way as privileged beneficiaries of the kingdom of God; they have a very special title to hearing the gospel, the "good news" of the coming of the kingdom. We shall

25

inquire about the basis, the *raison d'etre,* of this privilege. Fourth and finally, we shall recall the demands for renunciation and detachment from the things of this earth. Even though the word is not used, these demands bring us in practice to a real and effective poverty.

I. *The Needy*

A. *Vocabulary*

The term generally used in the gospels to indicate those whom we call "the poor" is *ptōchos.* It occurs 24 times in the gospels (Mt—5, Mk—5, Lk—10, Jn—4) and not at all in Acts. To this we can add one occurrence of the adjective *penichros.* In speaking of the "poor widow," Lk 21:2 substitutes this for the *ptōchos* of Mk 12:42. Finally, *endeēs,* "needy," occurs in Acts 4:34.

These "poor" appear above all as those in relation to whom we define and recognize our obligation of giving alms. Jesus tells the rich man, "Go and sell what you have and give to the poor" (Mk 10:21; Mt. 19:21; Lk 18:22). When a woman in Bethany anointed Jesus with costly perfume, some of the bystanders criticized: "It could have been sold for over three hundred silver pieces and the money given to the poor." "The poor," Jesus replied, "you will always have with you, and you can be generous to them whenever you wish" (Mk 14:5, 7; Mt 26:9, 11; Jn 12:5, 6, 8). Zacchaeus told the Lord that he was going to give half of his belongings to the poor (Lk 19:8), and when Judas left the upper room, the others thought that he was going out to give something to the poor (Jn 13:29). The "poor Lazarus" of the parable (Lk 16:20, 22) is described as a miserable beggar who was eager to gather whatever fell from the rich man's table. The case of the "poor widow" is similar (Mk 12:42-43; Lk 21:2-3); she takes from her own want to put two coins in the treasury. Finally, Acts 4:34 tells us of the first Christians, "nor was there anyone needy among them"; that is, no one lacked anything that was necessary.

We shall come back to the five texts which speak of the privilege the poor enjoy in relation to the kingdom. For now, we can affirm that in twenty-one of twenty-six instances "the poor" are simply those who are in need, people who must be helped. We recognize them again in the saying of 1 Jn 3:17; "I ask you, how can God's love survive in a man who has enough of this world's goods yet closes his heart to his brother when he sees him in need (*chreian echonta*)?"

The texts we have just cited obviously imply no idealization of poverty. They view the poor strictly from an economic point of view as unfortunate people who are in need of material help.

B. *The Duty of Almsgiving*

The picture of the poor presented by our texts is completed by various precepts expressly concerned with almsgiving. Matthew presupposes such a precept when he warns us against being ostentatious when we give alms (6:2-4), but it is above all Luke who presents this duty to us with special insistence. "But if you give what you have as alms, all will be wiped clean for you" (11:41); "Sell what you have and give alms. Get purses for yourselves that do not wear out, a never-failing treasure with the Lord" (12:33). It is Luke, too, who cites the example of Peter and John in relation to the crippled man begging alms at the temple gate called "the Beautiful" (Acts 3:1-10), and the story of Tabitha (9:36-43) and of Cornelius, the centurion (10:2, 4, 31). He also reports how Paul went up to Jerusalem to bring alms to his own people

(24:17).

Even where the expression "giving alms" is not used, generosity is clearly expected of Jesus' disciples. John the Baptist had already invited his hearers, "Let the man with two coats give to him who has none. The man who has food should do the same" (Lk 3:11). Jesus asks that we give to all who beg from us (Lk 6:30), that we lend without expecting repayment (6:34, 35), that we give without counting the cost (6:38). He invites us to "make friends for yourselves through your use of this world's goods, so that when they fail you, a lasting reception will be yours" (16:9). Luke further cites the example of the holy women who were assisting the apostolic group out of their own means (8:3), and the Christians of Antioch who were sending help to Jerusalem (Acts 11:29), and that of Paul, who worked hard in order to help the weak (20:34-35).

The care and concern which we must have for all the poor and dispossessed is nowhere recommended as strongly as in Matthew's description of the last judgment, with which he brings Jesus' public ministry to a close. "For I was hungry and you gave me food, I was thirsty and you gave me drink. I was a stranger and you welcomed me, naked and you clothed me. I was ill and you comforted me, in prison and you came to visit me . . . as often as you did it for one of my least brothers, you did it for me" (Mt 25:35-46). The Sovereign Judge considers the weak and unfortunate as his brothers and sisters; whatever is done for them is done for him. Is it possible to make us understand more clearly the importance of our obligations toward all categories of "the poor"?

So we simply cannot be a Christian without the practice of charity. This, however, can take different forms. One of these—the gospel insists on its necessity—is the forgiveness of injuries. Recall the fifth request of the Our Father, "Forgive us our trespasses as we forgive those who trespass against us." As for people in need, the Christian has the duty, no less urgent, of helping them with material possessions. It is clear that poverty presented in this way, as an appeal to our generosity, does not constitute an ideal. It is an evil, and we must try to relieve its victims.

II. *The Community of Goods*

A. *The Texts*

In several places in Acts, the author wishes to present overviews of the life of the first Christian community. The texts dealing with the common sharing, the community of goods, practiced by the infant Church in Jerusalem, occur in two of these "summaries" or "resumé" scenes.

After recounting the event of Pentecost and the numerous conversions which occurred on that day (Acts 2:1-41), Luke presents the first summary (2:42-47) dealing with the community life of these converts:

> [42] They devoted themselves to the apostles' instruction and the communal life, to the breaking of bread and the prayers. [43] A reverent fear overtook them all, for many wonders and signs were performed by the apostles. [44] Those who believed shared all things in common; [45] they would sell their property and goods, dividing everything on the basis of each one's need. [46] They went to the temple area together every day, while in their homes they broke bread. With exultant and sincere hearts they took their meals in common, [47] praising God and winning the approval of all the people. Day by day the Lord added to their number those who were being saved.

Verses 44-45 obviously overload the text at this point. Dealing with the community of goods, they anticipate the theme which properly belongs to the secondary summary and, borrowed apparently from there, were inserted here because of the mention in v. 42 of the communal life (*koinōnia*) to which the faithful devoted themselves.

The summary in 4:32-35 is properly concerned with the community of goods, an expression of the unanimity reigning among Christians.

> [32] The community of believers were of one heart and one mind. None of them ever claimed anything as his own; rather, everything was held in common. [33] With power the apostles bore witness to the resurrection of the Lord Jesus, and great respect was paid to them all; [34] nor was there anyone needy among them, for all who owned property or houses sold them and donated the proceeds. [35] They used to lay them at the feet of the apostles to be distributed to everyone according to his need.

Here too, an extraneous element has slipped in. Verse 33 speaks of the miraculous power exercised by the apostles and thus anticipates the theme proper to the third summary in 5:12-16. The basic text, then, is 4:32, 34-35, and 2:44-45 is an anticipated echo, a foreshadowing of this.

We must take note of one more detail: the summary of chapter 4 seems to have been planned as an introduction to the two incidents which follow. The first reports the edifying example of Barnabas, who sold a farm he owned and gave the proceeds to the apostles (4:36-37). The second concerns Ananias and Sapphira (a much less edifying example), who, when they had sold their property, donated to the apostles only a part of the proceeds (5:1-11). Peter explicitly tells the guilty husband, "Was it not yours as long as it remained unsold? Even when you sold it, was not the money still yours?" (5:4). Ananias was not obliged to sell his property, nor was he obliged to give any of it, either all or part, to the apostles. His sin consisted in this: he willingly lied (5:3). He pretended to give all, when in fact he had kept part for himself.

This episode gives us a clear indication that the putting of goods in common was in no way an obligation. This is presupposed also in the example of Barnabas. His gesture was worthy of mention only because it witnessed to an exceptional generosity. A little further in Acts we are told that Peter "went to the house of Mary, the mother of John (also known as Mark), where many others were gathered in prayer" (12:2). There is no reason whatever to suppose that this woman should have been reproached for not having sold her house.

When we return to our summaries after studying these examples, we cannot help but be struck by the difference in tone. Cases which were reported because they were outstanding examples have here become the general rule. "Nor was there anyone needy among them, for all who owned property or houses sold them and donated the proceeds. They used to lay them at the feet of the apostles to be distributed to everyone according to his need" (4:34-35). "Those who believed shared all things in common; they would sell their property and goods, dividing everything on the basis of each one's need" (2:44-45). We cannot escape the impression that affirmations such as these have generalized actions which quite probably remained exceptional.

While we can discuss to what extent these descriptions correspond to actual facts, this really is a bit beside the point. These summaries on the sharing of goods at Jerusalem receive their true meaning if we keep clearly in mind the author's intention in writing them. In attributing to all Christians of the early Church a generosity which in fact was found only in some, Luke wished to keep before his readers a model and an ideal which should always inspire the Christian community. Members of religious orders therefore have

rightly found here a form of Christian life whose perm-
ament presence in the Church they help to assure.
Faithful Chrsitians need to find in their midst the
practical realization of an ideal which the ordinary
conditions of life do not permit them to realize fully
in their actions.

But what exactly is this ideal? Is it one of poverty?
This is the question we now have to put to our texts.

B. The Ideal

The sharing of goods in the primitive Church presents us with an ideal. This appears first in certain
expressions chosen by Luke and by what these expressions would call to mind in his readers. He writes,
"Those who believed shared all things in common"
(2:44); "everything was held in common" (4:32). Reading this, how could his Greek readers not have thought
of the well-known saying, "Among friends, everything
is in common"?[1] He writes also; "None of them ever
claimed anything as his own" (4:32). This corresponds
to the proverb "Friends have nothing of their own."
In 4:32 we also find, "The community of believers
were of one heart and one mind." For the Greeks,
friendship consisted precisely in being "one soul."

In describing the church in Jerusalem, therefore, Luke
seems to have been inspired by the Greek theme of
friendship. He hoped to make his readers see that the
union of the first Christians was a marvelous realization
of the ideal of friendship that was already familiar to
them. According to this ideal, friends shared all their
goods, not in the sense that they renounced what they
possessed but rather that they put their goods at the
disposal of their friends. It is clear that this ideal of
authentic friendships points us not toward an ideal of
poverty but toward an ideal whose Christian name is
love.

Luke's descriptions of the Christian community call to mind the theme of friendship. We should not, however, view this as a casual reference. Another path leads us to the same conclusion. The statement in 4:34, "nor was there anyone needy among them," contains an allusion to Dt 15:4: "Since the Lord, your God, will bless you abundantly in the land he will give you to occupy as your heritage there should be no one of you in need." The Hebrew text contains a recommendation; Jewish tradition, however, tended to see in it a promise. This is perhaps already the meaning in the Septuagint, which uses a future tense, "For there shall not be a needy person among you for the Lord, your God, will bless you." This is even clearer in the Palestinian Targum, "If you apply yourselves to the precepts of the Law, there will not be anyone needy among you because the Lord, your God, will bless you." This promise of Deuteronomy finds its fulfillment precisely in the first Christian community: "nor was there anyone needy among them." If Christians therefore, put their goods in common, they do not do this to make themselves poor, that is, out of love for an ideal of poverty; they share so that there might not be any more poor. Again, the ideal is one of love, true love of the poor.

From our texts (2:45, 4:35), we can conclude that each had what was necessary according to his or her needs. In the church, no one need suffer poverty any more. Is it really correct to call such a community "the church of the poor"? (A. George, p. 402).

Finally, it is important to observe that the sharing of goods must not be isolated from a deeper sharing, of which it is only one expression. The summary in chapter 4 begins with the remark, "The community of believers were of one heart and of one mind" (4:32). The unity of Christians is founded on the one, the same faith and first translates itself into a union of spirit. It was to indicate this level of sharing that Luke was at pains to underline the unanimity (*homothymadon*) of believers when they gathered together before God at the temple (2:46, 5:12), or when they all prayed together (1:14, 4:24). Viewed in the same perspective, the sharing of goods can be related to the perseverance in "communion" that was characterized by the teaching of the apostles, the celebration of the breaking of bread, and prayers (2:42). Putting goods in common is only one consequence of the awareness that Christitans must form together (*epi to auto*) a single community, one body, in which each one knows that he or she is in solidarity with all.

We have now seen enough to conclude that the ideal proposed by Luke in his descriptions of the primitive community is neither that of poverty nor detachment but, more simply and more profoundly, that of fraternal love. This translates itself not into a love of poverty but into a love of the poor; it urges us not to make ourselves poor, but to watch carefully so that no one should be poor.

III. *The Privilege of the Poor*

A. *The Texts*

Of the twenty-four occurrences of *ptōchos* in the gospels, we have five instances left to examine. The first is in a citation of Isa 61:1 which is proper to Luke. Jesus' response to the disciples of John the Baptist (Mt 11:5, Lk 7:22) alludes to this same passage of Isaiah. Finally, we shal l have to discuss the first beatitude of the Sermon on the Mount (Mt 5:3; Lk 6:20).

1. The preaching of Jesus in the synagogue of Nazareth constitutes, in the gospel of Luke, almost a program of Jesus' ministry and is at least as important as Peter's programmatic discourse on the day of

Penetecost (Acts 2:1-41). Lk 3:4-6 defines the ministry of John the Baptist in the light of the oracle in Isa 40:3-5, "A herald's voice in the desert, crying, 'Make ready the way of the Lord.'" In the same way, the oracle of Isa 61:1-2, which Jesus reads to his compatriots, defines the ministry of Jesus:

> The spirit of the Lord is upon me; therefore he has anointed me. He has sent me to bring glad tidings to the poor, to proclaim liberty to captives, recovery of sight to the blind, and release to prisoners, to announce a year of favor from the Lord.

When he comments "Today this Scripture passage is fulfilled in your hearing" (4:21), Jesus identifies himself with the messenger who was announced by the prophet. At the same time, he makes us understand that his mission concerns the unfortunate; he must proclaim to them the end of their suffering.

2. When John the Baptist sent some of his disciples to Jesus, asking "Are you he who is to come?" Jesus replied,

> Go back and report to John what you hear and see: the blind recover their sight, cripples walk, lepers are cured, the deaf hear, dead men are raised to life, and the poor have the good news preached to them [Mt 11:4-5; Lk 7:22].

This response, consisting of a series of allusions to various oracles of consolation in the book of Isaiah, serves a double purpose: it enables John to recognize that Jesus' ministry brings to fulfillment the promises concerning the messianic era; then it helps him to modify his understanding of the task of the Messiah. John had threatened his hearers with the coming of the terrible judge on the day of wrath (Mt 3:7-12; Lk 3:7-9, 15-17) whereas, Jesus presents his ministry as a manifestation of God's mercy toward the weak and infirm. Jesus lists a series of miracles, including even resurrection from the dead.

The last sign, the one specific and decisive in providing the characteristic trait of his mission, refers to Isa 61:1: "the poor have the good news preached to them." Even more than by working miracles, Jesus gives the surest guarantee for recognizing him as God's messenger by bringing good news to the poor.

3. The beatitudes of the Sermon on the Mount have come down to us in two different forms which seem to derive from a common source. The first three, beatitudes form a unity, which, in the tradition prior to their being edited into the gospels, must have been somewhat like this:

> Blessed are the poor, for the kingdom of God is theirs. Blessed are the afflicted, for they shall be consoled. Blessed are the hungry, for they shall be filled.
> [Mt 5:3, 6; Lk 6:20-21].

If we are to grasp its true meaning, this text too must be seen in the light of the promises of Isaiah, and especially the oracle of 61:1-3, speaking of the messenger sent by God to announce good news to the poor, he announces, "Blessed are the poor for the kingdom of God is theirs!" This is precisely the content of the good news promised to the poor: the kingdom of God is theirs. We shall return to this shortly, but first we must ask if the "poor", spoken of in this context, are still the needy whom the gospels generally call *ptōchoi*.

B. *The Poor*

The question of the identity of the poor deserves our attention because of a particular "moralizing" exegesis which refuses to see in them people out of favor from an economic or social point of view. We are thinking in particular of explanations such as that proposed by A. Gelin:

> Does this mean that we must believe that Jesus "beatified a social class"? Has the Gospel any of the characteristics of a social manifesto? It canonizes no sociological state, nor places it in direct relation with the kingdom. A spiritual gift can be suitably received only in a spiritual situation. Only trusting faith can open man to God's grace. It is this openness to God that is called spiritual poverty.[2]

Since Jesus promises the happiness of heaven, he could not be addressing himself to people who are poor or hungry in the usual sense of these terms. In what way would these states be meritorious for heaven? And did not Jesus address himself to the small property owners? The "poor" of whom he spoke, then, are the "clients" of Yahweh who are open to God in the confidence of their faith. The "poor" to whom the gospel is proclaimed would be "poor", therefore, not by their economic or social condition but by their spiritual dispositions.

The texts immediately raise an objection against these explanations: at the same time that they mention the poor, the beatitudes include the afflicted (those who mourn) and the hungry. The oracle of Isaiah cited in Luke 4 associates them with prisoners, the blind, and the oppressed. The reply to John the Baptist also mentions the blind, the deaf, cripples, lepers, and even the dead. On the evidence, it would be difficult to spiritualize these terms as some do with the term "poor." Jesus announced the good news to people who were in distress, and this good news means for them, concretely, that their distress is at an end. The context, then, does not allow us to spiritualize the idea of poverty.

But what of Matthew and the form of the beatitudes in his gospel? The first is addressed no longer to the

"poor" but to the "poor in spirit," while the third
no longer concerns those who "hunger" but those
"who hunger and thirst for justice." Here we are on
a completely different level; Matthew is obviously concerned with spiritual dispositions. This point of view
leads him to repeat the beatitude of the persecuted. It
is not the persecuted, as such, who are called blessed,
but those who "suffer persecution for justice's sake
(5:10), those who suffer calumny without having done
anything wrong (5:11).

We find the same process in the first beatitude.
Sensitive to the religious overtones of the word *'ănā-
wîm,* underlying the Greek *ptochoi,* Matthew makes them
explicit by speaking first of the "poor in spirit" and
then of the "meek." If, following the Hebrew, "poor
in spirit" designates humble people, Matthew's first
two beatitudes correspond to his description of Jesus
as "meek and humble of heart" (11:29).

This spiritual reinterpretation of the first evangelist
is confirmed by other texts he has retouched in the
same way. In general, we can report that in texts
which speak of "the poor," Matthew speaks of those
who are "poor in spirit" and "meek."

Apart from Matthew, we believe that we must seek
the reason for the privilege accorded the poor in regard to the kingdom not in a completely gratuitous
analysis of the psychology of the poor but rather in the
content of the good news which is announced to them.

C. The Good News of the Kingdom of God

We have already seen that the theme of proclaiming good news (*euangelizomai*) to the poor is found in
Isaiah. Let us recall in particular the well-known oracle
of Isa 52:7:

> How beautiful upon the mountains are the feet of him who
> brings glad tidings, announcing peace, bearing good news,

announcing salvation and saying to Zion, "Your God rules (NAB: is king)."

The expression "your God rules" attributes an action too directly to God and would have presented problems to the Jews of the first century. The Targum employs the more respectful circumlocution "The kingdom of your God has appeared." When this kingdom is inaugurated, one can say "For the Lord comforts his people and shows mercy to his afflicted" (Isa 49:13). The kingdom of God forms the object of the good news. Let us cite another text, Micah 4:6-7:

> On that day, says the Lord, I will gather the lame, and I will assemble the outcasts and those whom I have afflicted. I will make of the lame a remnant and of those driven far off a strong nation; And the Lord will rule (NAB: be king) over them on Mt. Zion from now on forever.

Again, the Aramaic Targum avoids the direct expression "Yahweh will rule," and says "The kingdom of Yahweh will appear to them." This is the kingdom whose coming Jesus proclaims, and this is the good news he announces especially to the poor.

To see just how this good news particularly concerned the poor, we must enter into the thought-world of the Bible and ancient Near East and see what kind of ideas the "kingdom of God" would have called to mind; we cannot separate the phrase from the ideal of royalty which Israel shared with other peoples of the ancient world.

From the third millennium B.C., in Mesopotamia as well as in Egypt, the basic function of the king was to assure justice to his subjects. In exercising this prerogative, the king must take into account the concrete situation: among his subjects were the powerful and the weak, the rich and the poor. If things followed their natural bent, the rich and powerful would have

always tended to abuse their position in order to
oppress and exploit the weak and the poor, who, unable to defend themselves, would have been forced
more and more into greater misery. It devolved, then,
upon the king to reestablish equilibrium. By his office,
he was the defender of those who were unable to
defend themselves; he was the appointed protector of
the poor, the widow, the orphan, the oppressed. Justice, which he owed to his subjects, consisted in guar-
anteeing to the weak their just rights in the face of
the people with power, in restraining the rich from
harming the rights of the poor person.

In Israel, Yahweh was the king of his people and,
as such, the protector and defender of those who were
defenseless. His royal justice is here in perfect agreement with the compassion and mercy which are his
characteristics; all the unfortunates, all those in distress,
are the beneficiares of his attentive care. On the other
hand, we must not forget that the condition of the
poor in Israel was just as bad as in any of her neighbor countries. This was explained by saying that Yahweh, the king of his people, had not yet established
his kingdom on earth, but his kingdom would come,
and then he would fully manifest his royal justice. He
will "judge between the fat and the lean sheep"
(Ez 34:20); he will redeem his poor and will avenge
them on their oppressors.

From this perspective we can see that the announce-
ment of the coming of God's kingdom is good news
precisely for the poor and the unfortunate; they must
be the beneficiaries of this kingdom. The reason for
their privileged position must be sought not in their
spiritual dispositions but in the way in which God
conceives the exercise of his kingship. Blessed are the
poor, not because they are better than others, or better prepared to receive the kingdom which is coming,
but because God wishes to make his kingdom a shin-
ing manifestation of his justice and love in favor of

the poor, of those who suffer and are in distress.

The privilege of the poor therefore has its theological foundation in God. If we seek to base it on the moral dispositions of the poor, and in this way force ourselves to spiritualize their poverty, we are on a false path. The poverty of those to whom Jesus announces the good news of God's kingdom is seen as a humanly bad situation, making the poor the victims of hunger and oppression. It is an evil. This is precisely why the sufferings and privations of the poor stand out as an affront to the royal justice of God. God has decided to put an end to it.

The poverty spoken of in the beatitudes and the other gospel passages referring to Isa 61:1 is in no way proposed to Christians as an ideal. It is a situation which is revolting to God and is an insult to his honor. In order to give it positive meaning, Matthew must transform it into a "poverty of the spirit," that is, into humility and meekness. In this way the term no longer has anything to do with the very real distress it always evokes in the gospel; it has passed to a purely spiritual and moral level.

In proclaiming the good news of God's kingdom to the poor, Jesus manifests the care and concern which God has for them, his will to put an end to their suffering. From this proclamation, Christians must hold not that poverty is an ideal but that the poor must be made the object of a completely special love; in this way we share the feelings which God has for them.

The conclusion of this third part of our study thus coincides with the two previous parts: what the gospels and Acts say about the poor leads us to an ideal not of poverty but of love.

IV. Detachment

We have now reviewed the texts dealing with the poor. However, they obviously represent only one aspect of what the idea of "gospel poverty" means for us today. We would be seriously deficient in the exposition asked of us if we did not recall the existence of other large themes in the gospels, especially those which express the demands for detachment that Jesus imposed on his disciples.

A. *The Disciples*

Called to follow Jesus in his itinerant ministry, the disciples must have left their goods behind (Mk 1:18, 20; Mt 4:20, 22; Lk 18:28), *all* that they had (Lk 5:11, 28; Mk 10:28; Mt 19:27). The rich man, called to follow Jesus, finds himself up against the same demand (Mk 10:21; Mt 19:21; Lk 18:22); this too separates out those who present themselves to be Jesus' disciples but do not have sufficient preparation (Mt 8:18-22; Lk 9:57-62). How else could one follow "the Son of Man who has nowhere to lay his head"? (Mt 8:20; Lk 9:58).

The two parables of the man who is planning to build a tower and the king preparing to go to war (Lk 14:28-32) perhaps belong in this same context; they warn against attaching oneself too casually to following a master whose way of life implies a total detachment. In addition, there are the two parables of the worker who discovered the treasure in the field and the merchant who found a pearl of great price. They joyfully sell all that they have in order to buy the precious object and not miss the extraordinary opportunity offered to them (Mt 13:44-46). We can scarcely doubt that these two parables were directed originally to all those who heard the good news that the kingdom of God was coming soon; nor can we doubt that the early Christian communities knew that these parables somehow involved themselves, even if they were not necessarily asked to give up everything they had.

To Peter's remark "We have put aside everything to follow you," Jesus replies with a promise which goes considerably beyond the immediate context: it is addressed to anyone who, for his sake, would "give up home, brothers or sisters, mother or father, children or property" (Mk 10:28-29). The two parables, of the man who built a tower and the king who leaves for a war, conclude in Luke with a statement completely general in nature: "In the same way none of you can be my disciple if he does not renounce all his possessions" (Lk 14:33). They had also *begun* with very general statements: "If anyone comes to me without turning his back on his father and mother, his wife and his children, his brothers and sisters, indeed his very self, he cannot be my follower. Anyone who does not take up his cross and follow me cannot be my disciple" (Lk 14:26-27; cf Mt 10:37-38). Furthermore, the statement affirming the necessity of carrying one's cross after Jesus (Mk 8:34; Mt 16:24; Lk 9:23) is connected with a demand still more absolute in nature: "Whoever would save his life will lose it, but whoever loses his life for my sake will find it" (Mt 16:25; Mk 8:35; Lk 9:24; cf. Mt 10:39; Lk 17:33; Jn 12:25).

It is clear that the weight and import of statements such as these are not limited to the particular case of Jesus' own companions, whom he called to follow him on the paths of Palestine; they retain their import even after Easter. Christians in hearing them, hear the expression of demands inherent in their faith. Modalities can vary; one does not "follow" the risen Christ in the same way that one "followed" him in the course of his ministry. But "to carry the cross" is always the condition of "following after him." No one understood this better than Paul, thanks to the depth of his understanding of the Easter revelation.

"To follow Jesus" after Easter means to participate in the mystery of the "self-emptying" of Christ, who was reduced to the condition of a slave, making himself obedient even to death on a cross (Ph 2:6-8). It means, in other words, to share in the impoverishment of Christ. "For your sake he made himself poor though he was rich so that you might become rich by his poverty" (2 Cor 8:9). Christians know that, to share the riches of Christ, they must share in the mystery of poverty and self-emptying which he fully revealed to us in his death on the cross.

We should recall here the teaching of Paul. What remains more or less implicit in the gosple accounts emerges into full light, the light of Easter. Authentic Christianity exists only in sharing the mystery of the cross, a mystery of total obedience, even to death (Ph 2:8), to losing one's life (Mt 16:25, etc.), a mystery of poverty and self-emptying which he fully revealed to us in his death on the cross.

We should recall here the teaching of Paul. What remains more or less implicit in the gospel accounts emerges into full light, the light of Easter. Authentic Christianity exists only in sharing the mystery of the cross, a mystery of total obedience, even to death (Ph 2:8), to losing one's life (Mt 16:25, etc.), a mystery of self-emptying (Ph 2:7) in which Christ made himself poor, much more than we can possibly imagine (2 Co 8:9). A mystery—we can also include—of solitude, that terrible solitude of the cross, in the light of which our celibracy can be understood. We must of course add that sharing the passion of Christ brings us into sharing his resurrection. The obedience which delivers Christians to their God opens them to the transforming power of the Spirit; their emptying of self opens space for the riches of grace to fill; their solitude becomes the place of encounter with the living God.

The mystery of Easter therefore does not suppress the call to follow Jesus and the demands which that call entails. It is not a question of following him on the roads of Galilee or Judea, but of sharing in his self-emptying in order to share in his resurrection. But while this call is addressed to all Christians without exception, it can, according to the diversity of vocations, take different forms. The radical character it receives in the case of a vocation to religious life seems to constitute an indispensable element in the witness the Spirit gives to Christ in the Church. On this point we would do well to mistrust a certain juridical tendency which tries to found this particular form of Christian life on certain pieces of texts; its basis is much more profound: the very mystery of Christ, whose full revelation was made in the cross and resurrection. It is only if we start here that the call to a radical poverty, as well as obedience and celibacy, receives its true Christian meaning.

B. *The Missionary Instructions*

We now turn our attention to the instructions Jesus gave the Twelve and the seventy disciples when he sent them out as missionaries. He enjoined them to take nothing for their journey: "no food, no traveling bag, not a coin in the purses in their belts," not even a second tunic (Mk 6:8-9; Mt 10:9-10; Lk 9:3), "not a walking staff or traveling bag; wear no sandals" (Lk 10:4).

P. George notes that this is a beautiful example of "voluntary poverty". Yet we must not neglect the dialogue at the Last Supper, recorded in Lk 22:35-36:

> He asked them "when I sent you on mission without purse or traveling bag or sandals, were you in need of anything?" "Not a thing," they replied. He said to them: "Now, however, the man who has a purse must carry it; the same with

the traveling bag. And the man without a sword must sell his coat and buy one.''

The happy times of Jesus' ministry are over, when the apostolate was easy, when one needed nothing and lacked nothing. What would one have done with a purse or a traveling bag for provisions? But now, at the hour of Jesus' passion, a new period begins. Now one cannot do without a purse or traveling bag, and simply rely on people's hospitality. From now on, they can count not on hospitality but on hostility. The disciples, when attacked, would have to defend themselves; this is what the image of the sword suggests, which certainly has a symbolic value here.

This warning of Jesus can be a valuable warning to us against a certain literalism or romanticism which would lead us slavishly to observe prescriptions that were formulated in situation totally different from that in which we find ourselves today. Christians do not always escape the legalism that Jesus criticized so severely in the Jewish religion of his time. It is not the purse or the traveling bag that matters but a certain spirit, which we shall try to define.

C. *The Danger of Riches*

The gospel contains extremely harsh words addressed to rich people and to riches. The beatitude to the poor is followed in Luke by a "woe" which forms its exact antithesis: "But woe to you rich, for your consolation is now" (Lk 6:24). This woe is illustrated in the parable of the rich man and the poor Lazarus. We hear Abraham say to the former, "My child, remember that you were well off in your lifetime, while Lazarus was in misery. Now he has found consolation here, but you have found torment" (16:25). The reflections brought on by the departure of the rich man Jesus had invited to follow him are no more reassuring: "It is easier for a camel to pass through a needle's eye than for a rich man to enter the kingdom of God!" (Mk 10:25; Mt 19:24; Lk 18:25). "No man can serve two masters," Jesus says in another place, "either he will hate one and love the other, or be attentive to one and despise the other. You cannot give yourself to God and money" (Mt 6:24; Lk 16:13). Enslaved by money and the advantages it offers in the present existence, how can the rich man serve God and preoccupy himself with the future existence?

In the explanation of the parable of the sower, "those sown among thorns," are another class. They have listened to the word, but anxieties over life's demands, desire for wealth, and cravings of other sorts choke it off; it bears no yeild (Mk 4:18-19; Mt 13:22; Lk 8:14). Deceitful riches corrupt every thought. The heart of one who possess riches is attached to the goods of this world. So Jesus commands, "Do not lay up for yourselves an earthly treasure. Moths and rust corrode; thieves break in and steal. Make it your practice instead to store up heavenly treasure, which neither moths nor rust corrode, nor thieves break in and steal. Remember, where your treasure is, there your heart is also" (Mt 6:19-21; Lk 12:33-34). The rich farmer who thinks only of piling up riches to be enjoyed, even though he is going to die that very night, gives us an example that is not to be followed. The dishonest manager shows himself to be wiser (Lk 16:1-8). Here we can learn a lesson: "Make friends for yourselves through your use of this world's goods, so that when they fail you, a lasting reception may be yours" (Lk 16:9).

The temptation is to seek one's security in one's fortune; and the rich escape this only with difficulty. What an illusion! "Avoid greed in all its forms," warns Jesus; "a man may be wealthy, but his possessions do not guarantee him life" (Lk 12:15). To oppose this attitude, Jesus' disciples must divest themselves of all anxiety about the satisfaction of their needs, even the most basic; eating, drinking, clothing. In place of concern for all these things, in place of the security which can be sought in money, Jesus wants his followers to put their trust in God. He who feeds the birds of the air and clothes the lilies of the field more splendidly than Solomon certainly knows full well how to give these necessities to those who seek his kingdom (Mt 6:25-34; Lk 12:22-31; cf. Lk 21:34).

So here is the spiritual attitude which Jesus radically opposes to the desire for riches: trust in God. If it is true that we do not live by bread alone (Mt 4:4; Lk 4:4), Jesus knows that we cannot simply by-pass bread altogether. We should ask God for it, but not for more than we need for the present day: "Give us this day our daily bread" (Mt 6:11). And we should ask him with confidence, remembering that a father cannot fail to give good things to his children (Mt 7:9-11; Lk 11:11-13).

Jesus is not content to propose a seeking of poverty to counteract the instinct which urges us to accumulate riches; he goes further. He recognizes in attachment to money the expression of a need for security which leads us astray; so he invites his disciples to seek a better security with their heavenly Father, to place all their confidence in him, to depend only on his loving care. Jesus does not preach poverty for its own sake, nor even detachment in ragard to perishable goods; a stoic moralist could do that. The attitude of soul he demands of his disciples defines itself in relationship to God; it is essentially religious.

Once more we find ourselves far from what could be called an ideal of poverty. Having seen in the first three parts of this paper that the texts relating to the poor are oriented toward an ideal of fraternal charity, we affirm in this last part that the warnings against attachment to riches open on to the purely religious ideal of total and absolute confidence in God.

Postscript

In speaking of the demands which the call "to follow" Jesus entails, we had to face the qeustion: What validity do they preserve for Christians after Easter? It was Paul who, in what he says of the mystery of Christ's self-emptying, helped us see our way. "Though he was in the form of God, he did not deem equality with God something to be grasped at. Rather he emptied himself and took the form of a slave" (Phil 2:6-7), he who "made himself poor though he was rich" (2 Co 8:9).

We have studied these texts at greater length elsewhere (*L'eglise et la pauvrete*, pp. 343-55), but we cannot ignore the different interpretation P. Seidensticker gives them below. According to his interpretation, Ph 2:6-7 would say that "though he was in the form of God," Christ did not renounce this form but continued to exist in it after having emptied himself. He merely restrained it from prevailing in this life. In the same way, 2 Co 8:9 would mean that, while being and remaining rich, Christ made himself poor in accepting the human condition, which took from him nothing of his fullness of divine life.

In 1949 in (*Gnosis*, p. 99, fn. 1) we objected to a similar interpretation proposed by A. Feuillet. It proceeds from a deficient knowledge of Greek grammar—more specifically, of the rules dealing with agreement of participles. The idea of duration, which the use of the present participle implies, must be extended not in the abstract but in relation to the action expressed by the principal verb. In French (and English as well *tr.*), we realize immediately that "though he was in the form of God . . . he emptied himself" means an emptying which occurs when Jesus was, up to that moment, in the form of God. The same way, "being rich, he made himself poor" means that when he was rich (up to that point), he became poor.

Christ, then, really *did* renounce his divine riches, his divine "form." Obviously, this cannot be understood on the level of "natures," a perspective also quite foreign to Paul. His thought remains on the level of concrete conditions: Christ renounced his divine prerogatives. He could have reclaimed them, and, since the resurrection, he effectively enjoys them (which does not imply any kind of "disincarnation". In this context, Paul is not talking about the incarnation as such. We must take seriously what he says about the impoverishment of Jesus. Its measure was manifested not at the crib but at Calvary, for it is truly of the cross that these two texts speak.

Footnotes

1. In English there is a similar saying: "What's mine is yours." Trans.

2. *The Poor of Yahweh* (Collegeville, Minn.: Liturgical Press, 1964) pp. 107-8.

Bibliography Notes

This study rests essentially on a series of previous studies that it would perhaps be useful to recall:

Les béatitudes (Bruges-Louvain, 1954), pp. 141-148, 169-176, 183-223, 268-276. Second edition, entirely revised: *Etudes bibliques* (Paris: Gabalda, 1969), 1 :209-217; 2:13-142.

Second edition, entirely revised: *Etudes bibliques* (Paris: Gabalda, 1 969), 1:209-217; 2:13-142.

"L'ambassade de Jean-Baptiste," *NRT* 83 (1961) 805-821, 943-959.

"Les pauvres en l'espirit," in *A la rencontre de Dieu. Memorial A. Gelin* (*Bibliotheque de la faculté catholique de théologie de Lyon, 8*) (Le Puy-Lyon: Editions Xavier Mappus, 1961), pp. 262-272.

"Les ptochoi to pneumati de Matthieu 5, 3 et ‹anawē rūah de Qumran," in *Neutestamentliche Aufsätze. Festschrift für Prof. J. Schmid zum 70. Geburtstag* (Regensburg: Verlag Fred. Pustet, 1963), pp. 53-64.

"Annunciare la buona novella ai poveri," *Parole di vita* 11 (1966) 321-339.

"Eglise et la pauvreté," in *L'Eglise de Vatican II. Etudes autour de la Constitution conciliaire sur l'église* (*Unam Sanctam, 51b*), ed. G. Barauna (Paris; 1966), 2:339-372.

"L'interpretation des béatitudes," *Foi et Vie, Cahiers bibliques,* n. 4 (1966) pp. 17-39.

"La communauté des biens aux premiers jours de l'église," in *Etudes sur les Actes des Apôtres* (*Lectio divina* 45) (Paris: Editions du Cerf, 1967), pp. 503-519.

"Announcer la bonne nouvelle aux pauvres," *Charité* (March -April, 1969), pp. 6-9, (May-June, 1969), pp. 6-10. (July-August., 1969), pp. 6-10.

"L'union entre les premiers chretiens dans les Actes des Apôtres," *NRT* 91 (1969) 897-915.

As for other studies, we will mention only one, which we have already referred to: A. George, "Pauvre," *DBS* 7:387-406.

In addition to the above, we can add two more recent works on the subject by Dupont[*]: "Renouncer à tous ses biens (Luc 14:33)", *NRT* 93 (1971) 561-582; *Les béatitudes,* vol. 3 of *Etudes bibliques* (Paris: Gabalda, 1973), pp. 41-64, 153-203, 386-471.

The Call
of the Rich Man

Simon Légasse O.F.M. Cap

The Gospel episode of the call of the rich man (the rich *young* man, according to Matthew), appearing in chapter 10 of Mark and taken over by Matthew and Luke, presents us with a well-known scene. According to the text of Mark, a man approaches Jesus and asks him what means should be taken to have a share in eternal life. After making a point about the title the man had attributed to him, Jesus answers by recalling the commandments of the Law. "All these," the questioner replies, "I have kept since my childhood." "Then," the text continues, "Jesus looked at him with love and told him, "There is one thing more you must do. Go and sell what you have and give it to the poor; you will then have treasure in heaven. After that, come and follow me." The epilogue tells of a failure: "At these words the man's face fell. He went away sad for he had many possessions'' (Mk 10:17-22).

Since patristic antiquity, this scene and its dialogue have been considered one of the biblical bases for the monastic and religious state. To be more precise, the Matthean version of this passage particulaly provided the Fathers and spiritual writers with the gospel support they were seeking. Surely they found here the distinction between precepts and counsels; between the common Christian life and the state of "perfection." The version presented by Matthew does in fact seem to favor this type of interpretation. Here the supererogatory aspect of Jesus' second demand stands out in full clarity: after proclaiming the commandments, the conditioned call is offered. "If you seek perfection, go sell your possessions and give to the poor. You will then have treasure in heaven. Afterward, come back and follow me'' (Mt 19:21).

Nothing, it seems, could be clearer. Our authors would expand even further the *"si vis"* (*ei theleis;* "if you wish") in which they readily saw the expression of a call to depart from the common life by a voluntary and higher choice which was not imposed on all. So John Chyrsostom, for example, having listed the conditions of a true Christian life, continues in these words, "But when (Jesus) says, 'If you wish to be perfect, sell what you possess,' and again, 'let him who can take it, take it' (Mt 19:12), this is not a precept. He leaves it to the free will of the listener to do it or not to do it.''[1]

This exegesis of the passage can be considered "standard" if we are to believe its more recent commentaries, not only those of theologians or spiritual writers but even Scripture specialists. Some of them are quite astonished that Protestants do not perceive what others have judged evident and take a dim view of this interpretation. "It is amazing,'' writes Knabenbauer,

"to what subterfuges Protestants resort in order to
deny that these counsels, supererogatory works and the
state of perfection were taught by Christ!"[2]

Our intention is not to ridicule this interpretation,
which has been proposed even recently by some excellent exegetes and honored theologians, but to show
that at the present stage of our knowledge of the
gospels it can no longer be supported. The episode,
of course, still has its contribution to make to a
theology of the religious life, but it seems impossible
to find here an indication of two levels of the Christian
life, of two distinct states in the bosom of the Church.
It is therefore impossible to make this text, properly
speaking, the basis of the monastic or religious institution.

Before discussing the passage itself in its different
synoptic versions, we must recall several key ideas or
themes of the apostolic thinking. Indeed, contemporary
exegesis has acquired a sharper awareness of the role
of that thinking in the composition of the gospels
themselves. Further, the evangelists, while fully remaining witnesses of their times and milieus, appear
today as deeply pesonal writers and as catechists,
each having his own particularly favorite themes. These
they feel compelled to defend by rooting them in the
tradition. At the risk of anticipating a bit the study of
our pericope, it seems indispensable for us to set out,
here at the beginning, the essential data of the catechesis which the account of the call of the rich man seeks
to illustrate. We will do this very briefly, and for two
reasons: (1) We do not have enough time at our
disposal. This is plain. (2) Certain of these themes have
already been discussed in the previous papers. We have
in mind here especially the ideas of Luke on the poor
and on poverty[3] which we shall treat only insofar as
they appear in our passage itself.

I. Underlying Themes

A. Eschatological Detachment

The first generations of Christians were living in expectation of the end of the present era, the "consummation of the world," and of the act which would bring it about, the parousia of the Lord. But to live *in* expectation is not the same as to live *from* expectation. Opposed to a purely futuristic conception of salvation, Christians are still convinced that this salvation is already realized in Jesus Christ. For them, "this is the time of fulfillment" (Mk 1:15 and parallels), and the kingdom of grace has begun (Rm 5:1-2). This certitude brings with it serious consequences. The new covenant, promulgated by the apostolic preaching, is no less demanding than the old covenant. While the act by which God reconciled the universe in Christ is free and gratuitous in itself, to be effective it requires that humankind be faithful to the order about to be established. For Christmas, the only condition for access to the definitive kingdom they see coming on the horizon is that they conform themselves to it now. In other words, if we wish to receive Jesus as savior at the time of his second coming, we must be ready—we must begin now, in this earthly life—to live the relationships and dispositions which heavenly existence will crown at the time when the faithful will be "always with the Lord" (1 Th 4:17).

To express these dispositions, the apostolic parensis drew on a wealth of images and parables. One word especially expressed everything; "Watch!"[4] This call, rooted in the "light-darkness" symbolism that is common to both Judaism and the Bible, resounds through many passages of the New Testament because the first Christians knew that they were in no way already living in paradise. Their existence unfolded in "the night," constantly confronting the "Kingdom of darkness" (Lk 22:53). The dangers here are many. In addition to persecutions, which expose Christians to denying their master (Mt 10:32-33, 26:69-75, and parallels), we must not overlook the perils of a time of peace. It is in regard to them that we find the image of sleep used to designate that immersion in everyday life which leads us to forget the basis of life and to accept the yoke of evil and come to terms with pagan vices (Rm 13:12-13). It is also in this context that we find the corollary theme of vigilance or, better, the state of watchfullness, which encompasses a complete moral program that was presented for the practice of the disciples.

The exhortations to detachment, sprinkled throughout the New Testament, are also written within this framework. Here we approach our text, for these exhortations—among others, but more insistently—have in mind the peril which care for earthly goods presents for Christians. Paul was already convinced that "the world as we know it is passing away," and he exhorted "buyers" to "conduct themselves as though they owned nothing, and those who make use of the world as though they were not using it" (1 Cor 7:30-31). The commentary on the parable of the sower, in regard to the grain fallen among thorns, gives us the same teaching, but spelled out at greater length: "Those sown among thorns are another class. They have listened to the word, but anxieties over life's demands, and the desire for wealth, and cravings of other sorts come to choke it off; it bears no yield" (Mk 4:18-19). Thanks to a study of themes and vocabulary, we can recognize here—as exegetes have not always been careful to do—a common message that the Church was addressing to the faithful.

The same message occupies a good part of the

Sermon on the Mount (Mt 6:19-34), to which can
be added the parables of the treasure and the pearl
(Mt 13:44-46). Here, curiously, we find the same
formula is used as in the call of the rich man: the
two men of the parables are urged to sell all they
have so as to acquire the treasure and the pearl.
By comparing these passages, the call of the rich
man and the parables, we can suppose that Matthew
wished to concretize the teaching of these parables:
the value of the desired heavenly goods is so great
that, when acquiring the goods of salvation is in
question, we must not hesitate to sacrifice all of our
earthly possessions for them. This indeed is the conduct Jesus requires of the rich young man.

But how far does it extend? Whom does it concern? Must we believe that the evangelists, and
Matthew in particular, wished all Christians to despoil
themselves of their material goods and make the
Church an immense monastery? We are repelled
by the prospect of attributing to the evangelists a
project as utopian as it is disastrous. Still, we must
justify this repugnance in terms of the texts. Are not
these formulas quite straightforward? Did not Jesus
impose on his disciples, on those who wished to
"follow him," the obligation of leaving everything—
family and possessions?

B. *The Call to Follow Jesus*

Now we must consider a second theme, which we
will designate by the Latin formula *sequela Christi*
("the following of Christ"). This theme is expressed
in a group of texts which belong strictly to those
we have just brought forward and it views them
from the angle of their moral implications. This group
comprises notices, for the most part brief and extremely stylized, telling how Jesus called certain people

to follow him and leave behind their families and their goods. The call of the rich man is not an isolated example; we must study it together with a group including the call of the first disciples at the beginning of Jesus' public life (Mk 1:16-20 and parallels), the call of Levi (Mk 2:13-14 and parallels), and a series of anonymous callings, double in Matthew (8:18-22) and triple in Luke (9:57-62). It would take too long to study all these passages in detail; so we will content ourselves with some general observations.

We can readily admit that those ideas are rooted in certain historical facts. Although it is not easy to disentangle these facts from the schematization the passages have undergone, we are willing to admit that they all reflect the act by which Jesus called some men to leave everything to attach themselves to him, to share his itinerant life, to receive his teaching, and to contribute in their way to the proclamation of the kingdom of God. Distinct from the crowd, they deserve the name "disciples," just like the students of the rabbis, to whom they bear certain similarities. But they also differed from them considerably, because, first of all, Jesus did not intend to have them fill the echelons of the rabbinic circle— that is, to become rabbis in turn. It was enough for them to listen and do what the one and only master taught them (Mt 23:8).

On the other hand, Jesus required of them what no rabbi ever required of his disciples: the movement created by Jesus needed men completely free and at its disposal, dedicated at all times to the holy cause which he incarnated, ready to give even their lives for him (Lk 14:26-27, 33, and parallels). In regard to this, nothing was optional, for the conditions which Jesus imposed in the situation cannot be separated from the command to follow him which he addressed to these men. Either to refuse completely or to accept

completely: this either guarantees the eternal life of the
one who is called or compromises everything.

Let us add here that the group, constituted in this
way, was necessarily a small one. Can we restrict
it further and say thát those who were called belonged only to the college of the Twelve? There is
no gospel evidence that this was so; and if it were
the case, it would be hard to see why some of the
accounts leave such persons anonymous. Only the
first gospel has identified one of those who were called
with Matthew. So at any rate, the fact remains that
Jesus addressed the call in question, with the demands
accompanying it, not to the crowds of Israel but
only to certain individuals. The gospels testify to
this with sufficient clarity.

But it is likewise clear that in reporting these facts
(and others) the gospels are not simply recounting
events of the past; they are directed to the present
instruction of the Church. Now circumstances had
changed. If the words and actions of Jesus were to
keep their living force, it was indispensable to analyze
them with a view to discerning their profound and
permanent import, and in this way reply to the con-
victions and needs of the present Christian community.

Thus a rather different meaning came to be imposed
on what the term "disciple" had originally meant.
Far from restricting the term to the original close
followers of Jesus of Nazareth, the Christians actualized
it by identifying themselves with his disciples. From
now on, the "disciples" are the members of the
Church, not only for Matthew (where the term corresponds to a particular conception of the Christian
life) but also far the other gospels and Acts.

The same holds true for the behavior which
characterizes disciples. "To follow Jesus" completely
retains its aspect of personal union of life and death
with the Lord, but becomes dissociated, from then

on, from the specific conditions which originally surrounded it. The expression "to follow Jesus" comes to sum up in a phrase the commitment of those who hand their whole existence over to the will of the glorified Christ, who associate themselves with the community that unites them to Jesus' person, and who try to follow his wishes by remaining faithful to him even to martyrdom (Lk 14:27 and parallels).

Given this situation, from then on the demands of radical despoilment, which Jesus originally imposed only on certain ones, are addressed to everyone throughout the world who decided to be or had become a Christian. But then how should we understand them? On the one hand, these demands, concerning family and goods, would have quickly rendered Christianity quite impractical and even forced it to disappear; on the other hand, as far as we can tell from the witness of the New Testament, the apostles never imposed similar obligations on those who converted to the new faith. From these considerations we can suppose that these demands must be reinterpreted, just as they were reinterpreted earlier by the pen of the evangelists.

But we must do this correctly, and guard against the easy way out. One of the latter is to see here only a properly ascetic demand, a "counsel" offered only to *some* Christians, the most zealous or the most courageous. The general character of the idea of disciple is squarely opposed to this, as is the common understanding the Church has attributed to the expression "to follow Christ" in the gospels. It is not a question of a particular vocation but of the Christian vocation as such. Otherwise, these same demands present themselves without the least restriction, which would allow us to include them among supererogatory practices. Another easy way out, which we must criticize, is to seek to resolve the difficulty by restricting the application of these texts only to the individual case that was addressed by the historical Jesus. This approach which often seeks to understand the person who was called from a "psychological point of view," also fails to understand the purpose of the evangelists.[5] Faced with historicizing exegesis, we must affirm that, for the evangelists, these accounts have become paradigms, i.e., have acquired the value of a type and concern—not such-and-such a person who was encountered by Jesus in Palestine, but people whom Jesus meets and calls to himself today.

These two possible solutions lead us into dead ends. A final explanation suggests itself, one which has the merit of being inspired by the data of the New Testament itself. If we recall the zeal of the early Christian writers to warn belivers in advance against the dangers of riches, we might perhaps grasp the meaning of an order Christ gives to all, enjoining them to liquidate their possessions in order to follow him. If the formula Christ addresses to the Christian community sounds radical, it is because it originated in a situation quite different from that which the early Church was facing. The evangelists borrowed and used an expression from the tradition which in fact said more than they wished to say. Julian the Apostate, then, showed himself to be a poor exegete when he was inspired by these texts to confiscate the goods of the Church at Edessa.[6]

But does this view, which seems correct, go far enough? Does it exhaust the meaning of "despoiling" which Jesus, through the evangelists, demands of those who, then and always, decide to follow him? Should we not take more seriously the radicalism of these demands? It might be profitable for us to compare these demands with another teaching, which the first two gospels transmit and which appears twice in Matthew: the prescriptions concerning scandal (Mk 9:43-48; Mt 5:29-30, 18:8-9). "If your hand is your difficulty, cut it off! Better for you to enter life maimed than to keep both hands and enter Gehenna with its unquenchable fire." Following the common opinion, these formulas, with their brutal realism, can be considered only as metaphors to impress on us that every means, even the most serious, must be taken to avoid scandal, i.e., the lapse into unfaithfulness and the damnation which follows.

This, of course, is not exactly the same as the "call accounts," where the goods of material fortune, unlike the members of the body that cause scandal, cannot be considered symbolically. Nevertheless, this consideration aside, it seems legitimate to develop a similarity which the ancients, such as Clement of Alexandria[7], had already noticed and to which scholars today, such as B. Haring, have also drawn attention.[8] If possessions, by their attraction, place the salvation of their owner in jeopardy, the owner should not hesitate to get rid of all of them—to lose all in order to gain all. This would seem to be for us, according to the evangelists, the meaning of giving up all our goods, which Jesus, without the slightest limitation, requires of those who wish to become his disciples. The danger of riches is so great that no one wishes to take chances with them. Jesus declares to every Christian, and to everyone who wishes to become a Christian, "If you wish to enter into eternal life, and your goods turn you away from this, do not fool around. Go, sell your goods, and then you will have a treasure in heaven."

II. The Episode of the Call of the Rich Man

In view of what we have just presented, our opinion on the fundamental meaning of the episode of the call of the rich man should be apparent. It is, however, necessary to recognize certain distinctions among the three synoptic accounts so that we do not reduce them all to one common denominator. Presented first in Mark, the episode is reproduced fairly faithfully in Luke, but with several significant retouchings. Matthew, on the other hand, modifies the episode in a very personal way.

A. In Mark

We will begin with the oldest form, that of Mark. The episode cannot be studied properly without taking into account the whole literary context of which it is a part. Immediately following the call of the rich man, the author, seizes upon a closely related aspect of the story: as soon as the rich man has left, Jesus discusses with his disciples the dangers of riches and the advantages gained by despoiling oneself of them (Mk 10:23-31). This pericope, whose complex origins we cannot deal with here, sheds a special light, especially in its first part (10:23-27), on the scene which precedes the call of the rich man.

Restricting ourselves to essentials, let us examine Jesus' words on the difficulty a rich man has in entering the kingdom of God. For Mark, faithful here to the original futurist perspective on the kingdom, the kingdom is the definitive state, still expected in the future, and soon to be inaugurated by the parousia of the Son of Man. Viewed in the light of that blessed condition, riches constitute a very serious obstacle. Without doubt, God wishes to save the rich, for "with God all things are possible," but it is just as true that "it is easier for a camel to pass through a needle's eye than for a rich man to enter the kingdom of God." It would be wrong to emasculate this servere teaching by saying its object is simply a "spirit of poverty." To enter the kingdom of God, to inherit eternal life, this "spirit" (barring exceptions), simply cannot suffice. To be saved, one must, in *some* way, not be rich.

The episode of the call of the rich man, immediately preceding, serves to illustrate this teaching. But a serious change of perspective has taken place. The call, with its accompanying demands, has become a call addressed to all, and the rich man who receives it has become the type of every rich man who is faced with the call of Christ. Of course, that man has observed the commandments from his youth, especially those of the second tablet of the Law concerning one's neighbor—he has not even defrauded anyone, as Mark underlines by adding a prohibition not found in the decalogue. Still, he "lacks" one thing. The problem, which we will learn at the end, is that the man is rich, and riches and entry into God's kingdom are two realities which, if not actually incompatible, are compatible only with great danger. Jesus thus invites him to sell his goods and distribute them to the poor.

Despite an interpretation found among the Fathers, [9] the interest of the story is not on the poor in themselves. Mark is not presenting his hearers a message of social morality. The poor appear here only as the normal recipients of abandoned goods. The message is neither social nor collective. It concerns the individual fate of the Christian, faced with the imminence of the parousia. Riches in every instance are a formidable danger and must be got rid of, to the extent that they constitute an obstacle which prevents the Christian from watching for and receiving the Lord at his coming with the proper dispositions—in other words, whenever they impede the Christian from entering the kingdom of God.

The evangelist goes even further and extends his warning beyond riches. The story of the rich man is intended to illustrate any and every attachment to this world, which is passing away. In addition to riches, there is family. Even here Christ sees a possible obstacle to entry into the kingdom of God. Such is the message, similar to that of Paul in 1 Cor 7 on the advantages of celibacy, of the last part of the pericope (vv. 28-30). If Mark is eager to point out that breaking family ties for the love of Christ and the kingdom already finds compensation within the Christian community, he does not lose sight of the definitive "horizon," to which the Christian must sacrifice everything whenever this sacrifice is the condition of remaining faithful to Christ. The mention of persecutions (v. 30) highlights the precarious character of a reward still viewed in too temporal a way. Persecutions, the real test of faith, can come upon Christians at any time; they prevent one from becoming drowsy and dropping off to sleep, even within the peacefulness of the Church community itself.

B. In Luke

Let us move on to Luke's version of our story (Lk 18:18-23, 24-30). Because of Dom Dupont's treatment in the preceding chapter, we do not have to undertake any extended consideration of Luke's position in regard to earthly goods. It is sufficient to show how Luke, in incorporating this episode into his work, has marked it with his own stamp, but reflecting this same position. He does not radically transform the story; the essentials of Mark are found also in Luke. And some of his retouchings are surely the result of a better literary or stylistic sense. Other details, however, cannot fail to attract our attention.

First are those which involve Luke's parenesis on riches in regard to individual salvation. When he writes, insisting on the aspect of totality, "sell *all* you have" (18:22), he simply reinforces, as he usually does, the obligation Jesus imposes on those who wish

to be his disciples.[10] In the same spirit, he has
pointed out that the "first called" (5:11), and Levi
too (5:28), had "left everything" to follow Jesus.
Likewise, in a sentence certainly composed by Luke
himself, Jesus declares, by way of application of the
parables of the tower and the king going to war:
"In the same way, none of you can be my disciple
if he does not renounce all his possessions" (14:33).
This reinforcing is born of a keen sense of the dangers
of riches, which is evident again when Luke chooses
to omit the final clause of Mk 10:27, "With God
all things are possible." Thus deprived of that com-
forting assurance, the statement has a much harsher
ring to it; only the idea of the possibility of a rich
man's being saved remains. On the contrary, the
other two synoptics end with the idea of the all-
powerfulness of God; their message ends on a more
positive and more encouraging note.

In addition to changes which highlight Luke's moral
teaching concerned with the individual, there are
others which involve the community. Jesus tells the
man to sell his goods and give to the poor. In
Matthew and Mark the poor appear, according to
the custom of Jewish almsgiving, only as the beneficiaries of abandoned goods. They are secondary to
the essential act of giving up all to follow Jesus.
The same is not true for Luke; for him the duty of
helping the poor occupies a preponderant place. This
is why he has modified the order given by Jesus
to the rich man: for Luke, "give" (*didonai*) becomes
"distribute" (*diadidonai*), a fact we cannot help connecting with the use of the same verb in one of the
"summaries" of Acts, where we receive an almost
literal echo of our passage: "for all who owned property or houses sold them and donated the proceeds. . .
to be distributed to everyone according to his need"
(Acts 4:34–35).[11]

Again, the same communal point of view urged
Luke to make Peter's declaration in 18:28 more precise. Mark (10:28), followed by Matthew (19:27),
writes: "We have put aside everything to follow
you," In Luke, the phrase becomes "We have left
all we own (ta idia)," Here, too, Luke is echoing
the memory of the Christians in Jerusalem, none
of whom" ever claimed anything as his own (idion);
rather everything was held in common" (Acts 4:32).
In this way, the despoiling imposed by Jesus receives
an ecclesial dimension from Luke; it is placed at the
service of charity, which must unite the disciples
among themselves, following the pardigmatic example
of the first Christian community.

From this same point of view, Luke will retain as
essential the promise (in v. 30) of a "plentiful return
in this age," where the mention of leaving family is
set within the same communitarian ideal. On the
subject of heavenly reward, the evangelist did not
have to retouch his sources any further. The hope
of sharing eternal life pervades the whole story (18:18,
22, 30) and constitutes a further key element in
Luke's parenesis on the subject of riches. Let us simply recall that, for Luke, the despoiling of riches
for the benefit of the poor receives its reward in the
next life: "Make friends for yourselves through your
use of this world's goods, so that when they fail
you, a lasting reception will be yours" (16:9).

The promise of eternal reward does not apply only
to forgoing material possessions. Following Mark, Luke
extends it to the leaving of "home or wife or brothers,
parents or children, for the sake of the kingdom of
God" (18:29). Here too, Luke has not followed his
sources slavishly. In another passage, Luke associates
the detachment from family ties with the giving up
of material goods. In 14:25-33, Jesus successively
sets out three conditions for being a disciple, ending

each time with "cannot be my disciple." The three conditions are (1) to "hate" one's family (father, mother, wife[12] , children, brothers, and sisters) and even one's own life, if necessary; (2) to carry one's cross in following Jesus; and (3) to renounce all of one's goods in favor of the poor. The pericope is so well constructed that we are allowed to see a type of "catechism of the true disciple." Luke reproduces, once more, the sentence on carrying the cross (9:23), and in 12:51-53 he underlines the necessity of sacrificing the most valued attachments when fidelity to Christ is in question.

Luke is not a man of only one theme, and we find more in our passage then only an instruction on the use of riches; we find a catechism on the ruptures which an authentic Christian life is bound to demand in all spheres of our lives.

Finally, let us point out again that for Luke, as for the other two synoptics, the message of this pericope is addressed to all Christians. It is remarkable, on just this point, that Luke omits the departure of the rich man. In this way he seems to have wished to elimate any possibility of reducing the meaning of the episode to an exceptional calling, a supererogatory counsel. Indeed, the person effaces himself and is forgotten altogether. He is no more than the occasion for Luke to direct a moral instruction to the Church in its entirety.

C. In Matthew

As we have seen, Luke did not hesitate to make additions, subtractions, and other changes in putting his personal stamp on the story. His modifications, however, did not affect the structure of the story as a whole. Completely different is the personal work of Matthew (19:16-22, 23-26).

First of all, he has totally recast the episode of the
call of the rich man and given it the purely conven-
tional form of a scholastic or didactic type of dialogue.
This procedure is not unusual in Matthew, who,
like a good teacher, rewrites his sources with the
purpose of instructing his readers by putting them,
so to speak, into the story.[13] It is useless, therefore,
to try to find in this a more direct echo of the primitive scene. Furthermore, Matthew's personal intervention appears right at the beginning. The phrase
"Teacher, what good must I do to possess everlasting
life?" followed by the response of Jesus, "Why do
you question me about what is good?" is an obvious
correction to the parallel text of Mark, where Jesus
refuses to accept the title "good." Since Matthew end-
lessly exalts Jesus' privileges and divine transcendence,
such a refusal would not be proper for the Matthean
Jesus to make.

But yet another purpose comes into play. By this
change, Matthew situates the dialogue of Jesus with
the rich man on the moral level of accomplishing
the will of God. The question bears on "the good,"
of which God, who alone is good, is the norm. The
preoccupation of offering the Christian a complete
moral synthesis appears much more strongly here than
in the parallel texts. Although Matthew places particular stress on the Christian attitude toward earthly
possessions, we could speak of a small "Torah" for
the use of the Church. It is this, and nothing else,
which the dialogue of going to develop in three complementary stages.

1. The first stage consists in Jesus' reply to the rich
man's opening question: "If you wish to enter into
life, keep the commandments" (19:17). The condition for entering into eternal life is to live in conformity with the wishes of the "good" God. In
other words, it deals with rules decreed by God in

view of the good of his creatures; in particular, it
deals with the precepts of the Law.

2. We hear in these words an echo of the Jewish
faith, as it is expressed, for example, in this blessing
of the Mishna, "You are blessed, You who are good[14]
and who does good!" (Berakot 9:2). But Matthew
takes great care in adding a detail which constitutes
the second stage of development. It is introduced by
a new, purely formal question (useless to analyze
from a psychological point of view), intended to
awaken the attention of the hearer: "*Poias?* Which
ones?" (19:18).

These commandments are surely the same ones
which Israel had read in the decalogue from long
ago. Matthew, like Mark, is content to give a partial
extract from these ten commandments. But we must
notice that he completes his source by adding the
precept of love of neighbor, which is quite clearly an
addition (note how inelegantly the *kai* is attached to
that which precedes). Mark had already pointed in
this direction by citing only precepts from the second
tablet of the Law, but in Matthew the reference to
the Law becomes even more clearly a reference to
charity. This is far from being just a slight change
when we realize that, according to Matthew, the
Law, which has not been abolished (5:17), is still
offered to Christians, but with a content which goes
back to its essential principle, back to its source
(*ressourcé*). The gospel teaches this again in the dialogue
about the greatest commandment (22:34-39): reopen-
ed and reinterpreted by Christ, the Torah is a law
of chairty in which the commandment of love inspires and directs every action of human uprightness
before God. This is the second stage.

3. The third stage begins in verse 20 with a profession of faithfulness, "I have kept all these things."
Since the young man[15] affirmed that he had ob-

served the Law, as Jesus had reestablished it, Matthew could not have Jesus say (as Mark did), "There is one more thing you must do" (Mk 10:14). This is why, in Matthew, the phrase passes from Jesus' lips to those of his questioner in the form of a new question, "What do I need to do further?" In fact, he lacks nothing essential, and we expect that Jesus will tell him so and bring an end to the conversation.[16]   Nothing of the sort. Jesus in no way reassures the rich man about his faithfulness when he says, "If you seek perfection, go, sell your possessions and give to the poor. You will then have treasure in heaven. Afterward come back and follow me."

This meaning has been continuously exploited in the meaning we saw above, at the beginning of our presentation. It has provided the monastic and religious vocabulary with its most popular formulas: "perfection," "state of perfection," "perfect life." We must concede that appearances favor this usage; but these are only appearances. Nothing, in fact, is less founded than to see in the adjective "perfect" the idea of a higher form of Christian life, distinct from the common form imposed on all. We can convince ourselves of this if we take the care to examine this term in light of its context in the gospel and the religious environment of the period.

A first point to note is that, according to the Bible and the writings of contemporary Judaism, the two words, "good" and "perfect," are synonymous in their moral sense and both of them signify fidelity to the will of God. For example, in Ch 29:19 the "perfect heart" of the Hebrew text is translated in the Greek of the Septugint by "good heart." Still more clearly, the Rule of the community of Qumran (1:1–15) identifies the two ideas. "To do that which is good" is simply to "conduct yourself before his Face in perfection" and "to rule your strength according to the perfection of his ways." To be good or perfect consists entirely in the full observation of the divine prescriptions in the Law. Paul teaches the same thing when he enumerates, without the least distinction, "what is God's will, what is good, pleasing and perfect" (Rm 12:12). This indicates that, in the passage we are considering here, "to do what is good" (19:16) and "to be perfect" (19:21), far from dealing with different levels of life, are very likely on the same level, and synonyms.

The results are the same when we study Matthew. They are even more striking, since he is the only evangelist who uses the word "perfect" (*teleios*), and he uses it in passages which he himself is responsible for. Outside of our text, the word appears at the end of the antitheses of the Sermon on the Mount, "You must be made perfect as your heavenly Father is perfect" (5:48). Here, too, Matthew has modified his source. Luke's expression, "be compassionate" (6:36), is in much closer conformity with the preceding teaching on the love of enemies; it is also more at one with the biblical and Jewish tradition which, at that time, applied to God the notion of mercy. In this literature, the idea of perfection is directly concerned only with human conduct.

Matthew is thus responsible for the presence of both the term and the idea in his gospel. Since he would scarcely have changed its meaning from one passage to the other, the two passages must mutually illumine each other. "To be perfect" (5:48) is faithfully to accomplish the Law renewed by Jesus Christ, such as he has just defined and illustrated it in the antitheses which preceded. In effect, this verse closes all the previous teaching with a formula which sums it up wonderfully, since the very attitude of God is presented to humanity as the norm for a justice already attained and aways in progress (see 5:20). Furthermore, no one would dare maintain that this perfection and this justice are not demanded of all who commit themselves to follow Jesus in order to be saved. The same applies to the episode of the rich young man. Seen within its own context, as well as that of the Sermon on the Mount, the perfection required in 19:21 can be no other than the norm of all Christian existence as understood according to the Matthean Christ.

This universal and totally unreserved character of the idea of perfection is the same as that which the whole New Testament knows and which, without prejudice to the proper viewpoint of each author, agrees in its essential aspects with the viewpoint of Matthew. If at times "perfection" expresses superiority, it is only when the final and heavenly state of salvation is compared to the present, earthly state (1 Cor 13:10, Ph 3:12) or when "perfection" designates the normal Christian life, in contrast to an immaturity which we are are called to outgrow (1 Cor 14:20; Col 1:28).

We must conclude, therefore, that Jesus' words to the rich young man belong to this same common understanding, and the "two levels" of Christian existence find no support whatever. From beginning to end, the episode develops the same theme, deepening it step by step, whether we consider the end pursued ("eternal life," "treasure in heaven") or the conditions required to obtain it. To "do what is good," "to keep the commandments," "to be perfect" refer to the same reality and are imposed on all.

We must answer one objection which comes immediately to mind, Did not Jesus say, "If you wish. . ." and, by that, does he not indicate the optional character of the invitation? To point out the weakness of this argument it is enough to point out that "if you wish" concerns not the abandoning of goods but the perfection itself. Jesus did not say "To be perfect

you *may*, or if you *wish*, you'd *do better* to despoil
yourself of all you possess," but "If you seek perfection (wish to be perfect), go sell your possessions."
As we have seen, "perfection" cannot be placed
among the supererogatory means; is expresses the one
and only way of salvation. In saying "if you wish
to be perfect," Jesus is appealing only to the free
decision of human beings to commit themselves to
that, without the least nuance of being optional. Moreover, that formula has a strict parallel in verse 17,
which precedes "if you wish to enter into life," and it
cannot, according to all the evidence, signify the legiti-
macy of a refusal. "If you seek perfection" is copied
after that first phrase, and both of them, the work
of Matthew, express nothing other than two successive
aspects of the kingdom of heaven.

But what of the abandoning of goods which
Matthew, faithful to his source, seems to make an
absolute condition of obligatory perfection? Must we
believe that for him, fidelity to the will of Christ
obliges those who follow him[17] to rid themselves of
all their possessions? What we have said above about
this genre of demand suffices to put this question in
its proper light. According to the more general context
received from Mark (see Mt 19:23-26),[18] we can sum
up the teaching of Matthew in this passage in this
way: whoever wishes to attain salvation must submit
his will and his actions to the commandments which
Jesus renews on his messiantic authority. Such is the
perfection which makes of one a disciple of Christ
and puts him on the road to the heavenly kingdom.
The road is hard (see 7:13-14), traversing obstacles
and temptations. Sometimes the "scandal" becomes
menacing, so that at times the pursuance of perfection
demands courageous acts. Such is the case, above all,
for a rich man and his riches. By writing "if you seek
perfection, go, sell your possessions," Matthew completes

his teaching by warning Christians of the fullness of
their commitment.

Conclusion: The Scriptures And Religious Poverty

At the end of our study it would be useful to show
that even though there is no direct connection between
the religious state and the texts we have discussed,
these texts are not without relationship to the religious
state, as it has been lived and defined by the Church
throughout the centuries.[19]   We haven't space for a
complete study; so we will conclude with some brief
considerations.

In the first place, if it is impossible to found the
essential elements of the religious life (especially its
"armature," the three vows of poverty, chastity, and
obedience) directly in the Scriptures, these elements
are rooted there in a certain way. Religious life as
such was certainly not founded by Jesus, nor by the
apostles, nor by the authors of the New Testament.
But it is nonetheless true that this way of life gathers
together, and raises to the rank of an institution,
as aspect of Christian life to which the New Testament
attaches great importance. The gospel presents perfection as the goal to be attained by all believers,
without the least exception, by all the means necessary. In the scheme of religious life, however, one is
not content to use radical means only when the situation demands them but, instead, chooses freely to live
in a state where "the radical attitude becomes the
norm."[20]

The religious is marked by the absolute and, so to
speak, chooses to live in a state of urgency—not from
self-interest, or at least not *only* from self-interest, but
primarily from total involvement with the absolute,
with the kingdom discovered in Jesus, with Jesus
himself and all that he means and asks. Seized by

grace, as Paul was, and aware of its promises, those who commit themselves to this way of life wish to radicalize their lives to prevent any division of heart. They know that it is worth the effort. To borrow a saying attributed to Francis of Assisi, which could have been said through the ages by those who take the *sequela Christi* seriously: "So great is the good I have in sight that my every pain is a delight."

But again we must point out: the gospel reminds religious that they do not belong to a different and special category of Christian. The goal is the same for all, and if some choose special means, the *sequela Christi* and the perfection to which it leads are imposed on all and are possible for all, each person receiving from God the signs and graces which permit him to attain the kingdom according to his personal way; each person is required to take all the means necessary and face all the inevitable ruptures of life, when his membership in the kingdom is in danger of being compromised. There are not two classes of Christian, one higher, one lower; we cannot even say that there are two ways, one less good, the other excellent and infinitely more certain.

On this point, many of the Fathers and spiritual writers do not avoid a competitive spirit which comes close to a certain pharisaical pride. For the fact of the matter is that, in the order of means, the choice of the radical way is good and efficacious only to the degree that one has received the grace for it, i.e., a personal vocation. The way is good for *him,* not necessarily for his neighbor. The dogmatic constitution "De Ecclesia" of Vatican II very clearly brings out this personal aspect of the religious vocation when it speaks of "counsels voluntarily accepted according to the personal vocation of each" (6, no. 46-47).

The work of the Spirit certainly did not end at the close of the apostolic age. God alone knows if we are convinced today, as in the past, that the "Spirit of the Lord" swoops down on Christians with a violence capable of making Samson and Saul jealous. With the living Word of the gospel, could the Spirit not give birth to a blossoming for which only small seeds are implicit? That should not come as a surprise; the case, in fact, is far from unique.

What is left for us to do? A survey of the New Testament, enlightened by faith, is needed to revivify, even to rectify, some institutions which evolved later, after the "death of the last apostle," so that, having traced them to their origins, no one may stray from the essential paths.

Simon Légasse O.F.M. Cap.

Footnotes

1. *In Tit. hom.*, I:2 (*PG*, 62:666-667).

2. *Commentarius in evangelium secundum Mattaeum*, 2 vols. (2d ed.; Paris: Lethielleux, 1903), 2:164.

3. See the study of J. Dupont, above.

4. Mk 13:34-35, 37, 14:34-38; Mt. 24:42-43, 25:13, 26:38, 40-41; Lk 12:37; Acts 20:31; 1 Th 5:6; 1 Cor 16:13; Col 4:2; 1 Pet 5:8, 10; Apoc 3:2-3, 16:15.

5. For example, according to a very widespread pedagogical type of interpretation, Jesus wished to test a man whom he knew was attached to his goods in order to sound his sincerity.

6. *Letter to the Edessans,* in *Oeuvres complètes* ed. J. Bidez (Paris: Collection des Universites de France, 1924) p. 196.

The Call of the Rich Man 79

7. *Quis dives salvetur,* 24.

8. *The Law of Christ* (Westminster, Md.: Newman Press, 1966) 3:417; "La vocation du chrétien à la perfection," in *Vocations religeuse et monde moderne* (Paris-Fribourg, 1963) p. 98.

9. See Basil, *Hom 7 (against the rich), (PG,* 31:285).

10. See our *L'appel du riche* (Paris: Beauchesne, 1966) pp. 101-102.

11. See also Lk 11:22, where we can well imagine that the things that were stolen from the rich lord were "distributed," while in the parallel passages Mark and Matthew have nothing of the sort.

12. We can compare this situation to the one Paul evokes in 1 Cor 7:15.

13. Compare Mt 12:38 and Lk 11:29; Mt 12:48-50 and Mk 2:32-35; Mt 13:10 and Mk 4:10; Mt 18:1 and Mk 9:33-34; Mt. 18:21 and Lk 17:4; Mt 19:7 and Mk 10:4; Mt 22:41-46 and Mk 12:35-37.

14. Here this "good" or "goodness" is not an absolute attribute of God but rather of God insofar as he regulates his relations with his creatures in function of a plan that is in conformity with his excellence.

15. Jesus' questioner is presented as a "young man" (*neaniskos*), and this detail is proper to Matthew. This does not seem to be in any way an allusion to Essene institutions or to similar institutions among the *therapeutēs* of Philo. Most likely, we can explain this detail by the wish to attribute to the person the character of a student of the rabbis. In fact, other characteristics of their teaching methods are found in this text. As for the phrase itself, Matthew could have got the idea from the phrase in Mk 10:30: "I have observed all these things from my youth."

16. Origen (*Comm. in Mt,* (*PG* 13:1289-92) had already sensed the problem and proposed two equally debatable solutions: (1) the commandment of love was an interpolation or (2) the young man was not sincere.

17. "Come, follow me" must be interpreted in the context of Matthew not as an imperative in the proper sense, that is, as dealing with a distinct act of commitment to perfection, but in the sense of a purely logical succession: "then, you will be following me," "on this condition you can be my disciple."

18. In Matthew, the rest of the section (vv. 27-30) seems to be

connected more with what follows, while in Mark, and Luke, it is just the opposite: the whole section (Mk   10:17-31 and parallels) forms a unit.

19. On this see the excellent discussion of J. M. R. Tillard, "Le fondement évangélique de la view religieuse," NRT 91 (1969) 916-955.

20. *Op. cit.,* p. 932.

St. Paul
and Poverty

Philip Seidensticker O.F.M.

Preliminary Observations

A. Poverty and Riches

"Poverty" and "riches" are not absolute terms which always and everywhere have the same content or meaning. Their real content differs according to social and economic conditions, which obviously vary from one people to another. Where the standard of living is high, "poverty" can refer to a modest "well-being"; where it is low, "poverty" designates the minimum level of living, and modest well-being may be considered "riches." "Poor" and "rich," then, are relative ideas, simply two antinomic and complementary terms serving to define two opposed and mutually exclusive levels of life. They become meaningful only when specific, concrete situations make them clear and precise.

On the other hand, we must not forget that modifications in the structures of modern society have given birth to new forms of life which are no longer in harmony with the traditional understanding of the adjectives poor and rich. Since we propose to study Paul's position regarding poverty and the Christian community, we must frame the ideas "rich" and "poor" against the background of the social order of his period.

In antiquity, land, or real estate, was the basis of happiness, giving freedom, independence, and prosperity. Whoever found himself in a condition of dependence, even simply in the form of manual labor, had to earn his living and was counted in the category of "the poor." The idea of poverty, then, is the contradiction of "riches"; it designates the absence of riches, the privation of goods which guarantee the full development of the person; the absence of property, of the possibility of having the good things of life, of social and political influence, and of economic guarantees.

"Poverty" is a negative norm; "riches" is a positive norm.

B. Different Attitudes Toward Material Goods

Attitudes toward material goods differ, depending on one's conception both of humanity and of the world.

1. In *Ancient Greece,* poverty was not an enviable lot, much less an ideal of life. But from the time of Socrates on, the idea was affirmed that poverty and riches, therefore one's economic condition, are unimportant for one's true happiness. The only real value is "virtue," which leads to interior and exterior independence vis-a-vis the ups and downs of life, that is, which leads to *autarkeia.*

It is a natural response to place a high value on possessing riches; but the philosophy of the Cynics criticized this response strongly, going so far as to encourage profound contempt for all property in order to acquire virtue and interior freedom. The Cynic philosopher Crates spontaneously renounced a considerable fortune out of love for the virtue of personal *autarkeia.*

This independence and interior freedom, recommended by the philosophical schools, led the philosopher, quite naturally, to sobriety, renunciation, and disappropriation.[1]

2. On a religious level, we can discover another approach to poverty. Old Testament piety recognized in poverty a form of proper religious existence. The poor are pious people who cannot rely, as the rich do, on material goods or temporal influence, but root their entire existence in God; they orient their whole lives to him from whom they eagerly await their only salvation. In this perspective, poverty becomes a religious idea which does not necessarily include economic poverty.[2]

3. While the New Testament remains faithful to the idea of poverty as a form of religious existence (see Mt. 5:3ff.), it connects the idea of a tie that binds man to God also to the person of Jesus of Nazareth, the Messiah sent by God (see Mt. 5:11). The New Testament ideas on complete faithfulness, translated into an integral imitation of Christ, were based on the religious attitude of the "poor before God" that was typical of the Jewish world of the Old Testament but was enriched by various Hellentistic motifs. In the same way that Hellenistic philosophy taught that supreme happiness is acquired by the virtue of *autarkeia* through renunciation, or interior detachment from the goods of this world, Jesus, following the synoptic teaching, demanded of his disciples, in virtue of the

eschatological urgency, a break with all earthly goods and the renunciation of property for love of him.[3] We find nothing like this in the rabbinic tradition.

Hellenistic *autarkeia* is replaced in the synoptic gospels by a reality related to the history of salvation. The community of perfect life with Jesus is the only way to true happiness, to eternal life (Mk 10:17 and parallels) for man. Because the history of salvation now stands in the eschatological situation, the demand to give up all exterior goods "for the love of Jesus" is pushed to the limit and then connected with the rabbinic motivation of the "call to follow" the master.

C. *The Pauline Position*

It is not only an intriguing idea but a necessity to examine the Pauline position in relation to the idea of poverty. As this study will make clear, the spirituality of poverty espoused by the Jews of the Old Testament and the invitation of the synoptics to follow Jesus, which develops out of the former, are only one way of presenting the call to Christian perfection, a way which had acquired particular importance in the Palestinian communities of the primitive Church.

The Pauline (and Johannine) preaching leads the faithful of Asia Minor and Europe to perfect community with Christ along other ways.[4] Paul, a Jew by birth, is familiar with rabbinic exegesis (see Acts 22:3), but, being a Jew of the Diaspora, his thought and the formation of his spirit are also marked by the ideals of Hellenistic life. We can expect, then, *a priori,* that Paul will be closer to Hellenistic ideas than to the biblical spirituality of the Palestinian Jews who, within that pious milieu, were called "the poor." Further, Paul is a missionary to the Greeks, not the Palestinian Jews (see Gal 2:7-9).

Without wishing to anticipate the results of our

study, we can repeat a well-known observation: Jesus of Nazareth, in his earthly existence, plays only a minimal role in the Pauline preaching.[5] Pauline theology is directed to Jesus Christ, the exalted Lord, the *Kyrios*. In the same way, Pauline moral theology is nothing but the demands of the paschal Christ at work in the one baptized. Likewise, Paul lacks the perspective from which the idea of "following Jesus" in the course of his ministry could develop; the Pauline vocabulary does not even know the term "follow." In typical Hellenistic style, Paul speaks of imitating Jesus' basic attitudes (e.g., Ph 2:5), but more often he urges his communities to imitate himself: "Imitate me as I imitate Christ (1 Cor 11:1; see also 1 Th 1:6; 2 Th 3:7, 9; 1 Cor 4:16). The example of Christ is efficacious, therefore, only indirectly through the example of Paul, the founder and father of the community.[6] But the Apostle does not call the Christian to "follow him"; he does not gather disciples who follow his steps and share a community of life with him, as Jesus and the Jewish rabbis had done.

It is difficult to determine Paul's exact position relative to poverty; in fact, we can find no mention of this subject in his letters. The only exception is the passage of 1 Tim 6:6-19, where the author gives several reflections on the attitude of Christians toward riches and poverty. Here we will follow the wise and modest opinion of L. Cerfaux: "There is good reason not to use the Pastoral letters in truly erudite studies without due prudence, whether there is a question of defining the theology of the Apostle, or an attempt to reconstruct the history of primitive Christianity."[7]

We can treat here in substance only two themes: (1) the position of Paul in relation to social poverty and (2) Paul's refusal to let himself be supported by the communities. In dealing with the first, we will have to investigate the collection for the "poor" in Jerusalem, which Paul organized in his missionary areas, to see what information it can give and what its theological meaning is. The second theme deals with the particular character of Paul's personal renunciation. We will have to see from what theological awareness of his role this renunciation springs.

I. The Position Of Paul In Relation To Social Poverty

A. Linguistic Analysis

A study of Pauline vocabulary produces an astonishing result: the typical Greek expressions to designate poverty, *endeēs, penēs,* and even *ptōchos,* are completely lacking in his letters.

1. *Endeēs* means "in need, needing help"—or "poor" in our understanding of the word. This common term is well known to the Hellenistic Jews, Philo and Josephus. In the LXX, it characteristically translates the Hebrew *,ebyôn,* which forms the basis for legislation dealing with the poor. In Dt 15 and 24, for example, it occurs in four places (Dt 15:4, 7, 11, 24:14); Dt 15:4 states, "there should be no one of you in need." The legislation commands that one help and assist a poor person in need. Luke makes a clear allusion to this passage when he uses the word in Acts 4:34 (and only here) to describe the ideal situation of the community of salvation at Jerusalem, "nor was there anyone needy among them."

Again, the word does not occur in Paul. Although we must admit that there were still needy persons in his communities, nowhere does the Apostle refer to the biblical legislation on the poor.

2. *Penēs,* connected with the words *penomai* ("bound to work") and *ponos* ("hard work"), designates a man at work. Not only is it lacking in Paul, but, generally speaking, in the New Testament as a whole.

The LXX, however, is familiar with it. The absence
of the word in Paul is all the more surprising because
he speaks of the man who is obliged to earn his living
by personal work. *Penēs* indicates the economic condition
of the artisan, the day worker, who lives in dependence
on others. Paul, himself a tent maker, belongs to this
category of poor.[8]

3. Examination of the word *ptōchos* is of particular
interest. It designates the poor person who is reduced
to begging, totally deprived and dependent on the
help of others. This is the term diametrically opposed
to *plousios,* "rich." Between these two extreme situations stands the *penēs,* who resolutely refuses to be
confused with the *ptōchos.* While it is true that, according to Aristophanes, *ptōcheia* is the "sister" of
penia, the former describes a situation of much greater
misery. Plutarch defines each of them as follows:
"The life of the *ptōchos* consists in having nothing,
that of the *penēs* in being frugal and increasing his
resources through some manual labor."[9] Because
of the radical opposition between *ptōchos* and *plousios,*
the former became used in proverbs as the antithesis
of the latter. Thus "rich" and "poor" become stylistic turns of phrase in which the idea of "poor" has
long lost its meaning of being reduced to begging.
The primitive antithesis has become, in proverbial
language, an example of contradictory opposition.
The two realities, in a "formula of totality," now
embrace all possible forms of human life.

The LXX is also familiar with the word in its
primitive sense of begging, but prefers to use it to
designate the religious attitude of the pious before
God ("the poor": the *'anāwîm*). The New Testament
also uses it both in its proper sense and its relative
sense, referring to the biblical spirituality of poverty.
Here again Paul surprises us. He mentions the *ptōchoi*
only twice, and each time the word refers to the

"poor" of Jerusalem whom he must remember (Gal 2:10) and for whom he organized the collection (Rom 15:26).

The noun "poverty" and the verb "to be poor" are always found (contrasted to "rich") in connection with the collection for Jerusalem—in 2 Cor 8:2 and 9, where the passage concerning Christ ends with "how for your sake he made himself poor though he was rich so that you might become rich by his poverty." Paul uses the same rhetorical turn of phrase, "rich and poor," in another paradoxical statement in the same letter. 2 Cor 6:10, in a rather poetic description of his destiny as apostle, assures us that although "poor, we enrich many." With the exception, then, of 2 Cor 6:10, Paul uses the term *ptōchoi* only in relation to the collection for the "poor" in Jerusalem.[10]

This rapid survey brings us to the surprising conclusion that the idea of poverty, understood as a state of being in need, is almost totally absent from the thought of Paul. Only in connection with the word *ptōchos* do we have to look a bit more closely at his thought.

B. *"The Poor" according to Gal 2:10 and Rom 15:26*

In Gal 2:10, Paul affirms insistently that at the time of the Council of Jerusalem he and Barnabas had been given one stipulation, "that we should be mindful of the poor" (*tōn ptōchōn hina mnēmoneuōmen*)—to which Paul adds his comment, "the one thing that I was making every effort to do." It is common to see in this verse an allusion to the collection that Paul had undertaken in A.D. 57. That collection is mentioned for the first time in 1 Cor 16:1-4, where the Galatians are expressly associated with it. A more detailed discussion appears in 2 Cor 8 and 9 (and

perhaps also in 12:16-18). And finally, in Rom 15:25-
26, Paul informs his readers that he intends to go to
Jerusalem "to bring assistance to the saints.[11] Macedonia and Achaia have kindly decided to make a contribution for those in need (i.e., the poor) among
the "saints in Jerusalem." Here, again as in his recent
letter to the Galatians, Paul uses the term "poor"
in reference to Jerusalem. [12]

We now have to ask: Is the collection taken up for
Jerusalem connected in any way with the invitation
in Ga 2:10 to "be mindful of the poor"? It is not
at all impossible that, in his gloss ("the one thing
that I was making every effort to do"; Ga 2:10b),
Paul had in mind the collection which is almost
completed; but there are difficulties in trying to
assimilate the need to "be mindful of the poor,"
expressed by the apostles of Jerusalem, with the collection organized by Paul. In the first place, he himself expresses hesitation that "the offerings I bring to
Jerusalem may be well received by the saints there"
(Rom 15:31). And the lapse of time separating the
stipulation of the Council of Jerusalem (ca. A.D.
48-49 from the collection taken up by Paul poses
another problem. The latter began a full eight years
later, and was finally taken to Jerusalem only in
A.D. 58. No indication whatever exists that in the
preceeding years the Apostle had organized a similar
collection, besides this one, for the church in Jerusalem. [13] If then, the stipulation of Gal 2:10 is not
connected with the collection, the question is raised:
what is the meaning of this stipulation, and what
can the term "poor," which is used there, mean?

If we see a connection between the collection in
Rm 15:26 and Ga 2:10, the expression "the poor"
must be taken in its literal sense, social poverty,
and this is strengthened by the use of the same terminology in Rom 15:26, where the collection for the

poor of the saints in Jerusalem is mentioned.[14] The genitive, "the poor *of* the saints," can have a partitive sense in Greek, but it is also possible that "this expression indicates the manner in which the community of Jerusalem designated itslef," as in Gal 2:10.[15] The "poor" would be, according to the biblical spirituality of the poor, the "saints," the faithful of Christ in Jerusalem, the members of the community of eschatological salvation. In this perspective, the conjunctive genitive, "the poor of the saints" (Rom 15:26), is only the full and solemn designation[16] for what is expressed more briefly in Gal 2:10. It is likely that the recipients of the epistle to the Romans might have had difficulty in understanding this formula, influenced by the previous letter to the Galatians.

This interpretation of "the poor" as an honorary title of the Jerusalem community is further confirmed by the fact that everywhere else Paul calls the beneficiaries of the collection simply "the saints" (Rom 15:25; 1 Cor 16:1, 15; 2 Cor 8:4, 9:1, 12). Nowhere does Paul say that the community of Jerusalem is in need. It is just as difficult to imagine that the community, which at the time of James was enjoying the highest regard, would not have benefited from Jewish assistance to the poor; based on the Law of Moses, it was organized in an exemplary fashion. Acts further supposes the existence of a Christian organization for properly charitable work (6:1-6).

E. Bammel maintains that in these passages Paul is quoting, in some way, from the "minutes" of the meeting in Jerusalem, and borrowed the term "the poor" from there.[17] We can subscribe to this opinion.

Given the difficulty of connecting the collection organized by Paul and the request of the Council of Jerusalem, mentioned in Gal 2:10, we ask another question: Can "to remember" (*mnemoneuein*) have a meaning other than economic assistance?[18] The Greek

word corresponds to the Masoretic idea of *zakar* and
arises from grateful testimonies.[19] One "remembers
with recognition" the mighty deeds and interventions
of God in the Old Testament and, in the New, the
works of Jesus (see Lk 22:19; 1 Cor 11:24-25), as
well as those of others (Mk 14:9 and parallels; Jn
11:2, 12:3ff.). We can also "remember" those who
have transmitted to us the faith in Jesus. "Remember
your leaders who spoke the word of God to you"
(Heb 13:7). Here "remembering" takes on the meaning of imitating their faith: "Consider how their lives
ended, and imitate their faith." We find the same
association of ideas in 1 Cor 11:1-2: "Imitate me as
I imitate Christ. I praise you because you always
remember me and are holding fast to the traditions
just as I handed them on to you." We "remember"
those from whom we have received the good news of
salvation: we profess one and the same faith with them.

In the light of these formulas, the stipulation of the
apostles of Jerusalem to "be mindful of the poor"
(Gal 2:10) cannot have any meaning other than to
remind the church of the Gentiles, founded by Paul,
that it should recognize the Judeo-Christian community of Jerusalem as its mother Church and, through
"remembering," remain in communion with her.
Maintaining this unity between the church of the Jews
and that of the pagans was a prime preoccupation of
the apostles, and of Paul above all. He took this
"remembering" very seriously: Jerusalem is also the
mother Church of the community issuing from the
Gentiles.[20] The collection, organized some years later,
is only one of the ways of maintaining contact with
Jerusalem.

The term *ptōchos* in Gal 2:10 and Rom 15:26 is,
then, not Paul's *own* term but the expression used by
the Jerusalem church to identify itself. It shares the
religious motivations of the spirituality of the poor

as found in primitive Judaism, and for Paul it can scarcely be anything but an honorary title.

C. *"Poverty" and "Riches" in the Justification of the Collection (2 Cor 8-9)*

If the idea of *ptōchos* in Gal 2:10 and Rom 15:26 does not primarily include the element of economic and social necessity, we must justify our interpretation in relation to 2 Cor 9:12. Here Paul makes the incidental remark that "the administration of this public benefit not only supplies the needs of the members of the church (i.e., the saints), but also overflows in much gratitude to God." The current interpretation of this is that it deals with the alleviation of economic necessity. But the context of the phrase, which, according to H. Windisch, is completely disjointed and impossible to recover,[21] gives it another orientation and permits us to view it in a new way: receiving the collection will be an occasion for the saints of Jerusalem to glorify God, and for two reasons. On the one hand, pagans profess faith in the good news, such as it was heard in Jerusalem, and, on the other hand, the generosity of the Gentile community toward the faithful of Jerusalem is a sign and witness of its sincerity. The collection is a sign of the unity between Jewish Christians and Gentile Christians.[22] In the same way, "supplying the need" is a favorite expression in Pauline language, used to define the strengthening or perfecting of a community.[23] Paul sees, in the assistance given, a debt of recognition which pagans owe Jerusalem, for between themselves and Jerusalem exists the relationship of students and master, and here the principle applies: "The man instructed in the word should share all he has with his instructor" (Gal 6:6; see 1 Cor 9:11, Rom 15:27, and 1 Tim 5:17).

In justifying the collection at greater length in 2 Cor 8-9, Paul does not explicitly appeal to the spirit of community but seeks especially to stimulate fraternal love. The collection is a "proof of your love" (8:24); it testifies to "your generous love" (8:8). Paul asks them to give generously: "Your plenty at the present time should supply their need so that their surplus may one day supply your need, with equality as a result" (8:14; see also 9:12). The daughter communities therefore must help the mother Church from their material goods in order to receive from her an abundance of spiritual goods in returen.

Paul delights in using figures of speech, rhetorical turns of phrase, paradoxical and antithetic formulas (see below on Paul's "ideology of exchange"). He speaks with emphasis about the "plenty" and the "need" freely inverting these terms and bringing into mutual relationship their literal and figurative meanings. These antitheses are of a rhetorical character and give us scarcely any historical information. We can see an indication of this if we notice that in 8:14 Paul attributes a "plenty" in material goods to a community which, just a few verses before, he had referred to in an opposite light: "In the midst of severe trial their overflowing joy and deep poverty have produced an abundant generosity" (8:2). The reference to "poverty," here connected with the idea of trial, does not give us historical information either, but brings us closer to the domain of the biblical-religious notion of poverty (see Acts 2:19). Paul juggles ideas which, in the last analysis, always go back to rich/poor, but in his rhetorical style the terms lose their real value and must be understood in a larger sense. In rhetoric, they often keep only their emotional overtones.

What is most important for Paul is that the generosity of believers testify to the grace they have re-

ceived. 2 Cor 8 mentions the idea of grace no less
then five times (8:1, 4, 6, 7, 9): "Brothers, I should
like you to know of the grace of God conferred on the
churches of Macedonia" (8:1). The Corinthians must
make this grace bear fruit (8:4, 6, 7). In concluding,
these thoughts, Paul refers to the example of Christ:
"You are well acquainted with the favor (*charis*)
shown you by our Lord Jesus Christ." In what
does this example consist? "How for your sake he
made himself poor though he was rich so that you
might become rich by his poverty" (8:9). Paul again
takes up the proverbial rich/poor antithesis (e.g., "their
overflowing joy and their deep poverty have produced an abundant generosity"; 8:2), but it is used
now in the opposite way, connected with the history
of salvation ("theology of exchange"): from being
rich, Jesus Christ makes himself poor to make you,
the poor, rich (the play on words deserves to be
emphasized). The force of the idea undoubtedly resides
in the expressions "to be rich" and "to make rich."
Paul returns here to the original meaning of *plousios,*
the abundance of earthly goods, but, applied to the
supernatural world, it is clearly to be taken in a
figurative sense. "Riches" is an expression adequate
to designate the divine nature of Christ and salvation,
which is not accessible to men in its inexhaustable
fullness except in Christ. Christ is not only rich,
he enriches "all who call upon him" (Rom 10:12)
by making them share in his supernatural riches.[24]

The allusion to the incarnation of Christ ("he
made himself poor") does not have, in this case, its
proper signification; it concerns instead the mediation
of salvation by Christ, the communication of riches
of which the incarnation is only the first fruit. Further,
characterizing the incarnation by the expression "become poor" is intimately connected with the idea
of the divine "riches." The life of Jesus, begun

in the incarnation, was not, according to Paul, "poor" in the economic sense of lacking material goods—"for this is not the form of poverty which enriches those who believe in him" (Bachmann)—but in the sense that Christ renounced the riches of the glory of the divine world in order to live within the narrow limits of earthly existence, deprived of that glory, and, finally, to lay down his life. This "poverty," with its example of *kenōsis* ("emptying"), applies only to the particular situation of Christ. Even insofar as he is man, Jesus did not renounce his divine riches, but, "while being and remaining rich" (*plousios ōn,* in the present form), while retaining in his incarnation the fullness of life and salvation of God, Christ did not glory in that fullness of life and power and did not exploit it to his own advantage (see Ph 2:5ff.).

The point of the comparison proposed to the Corinthians is not, therefore, the imitation of the "poverty" of Christ, which is a figurative description of his incarnation, but the imitation of the *charis* of Christ, of that love which enriches others. This is why Paul introduces the example by noting that he wishes, by means of the collection, to test the sincerity of the love of the community in Corinth (8:8). Paul is not interested in impoverishment in the economic sense of "need"; rather, each should give according to his means (8:13); in helping others, no one should himself be reduced to need (8:13); "there should be a certain equality." Paul is not interested in economic poverty as such but rather in the efficaciousness of charity: "so that you might become rich" (8:9b).

D. *"Poor, yet We Enrich Many" (2 Cor 6:10)*

The "theology of exchange" (*Tauschtheologie*) is one of the favorite themes in 2 Corinthians: Christ "made himself poor though he was rich so that you might become rich by his poverty" (8:9); the communities enrich each other by their collections; the "poor" in Jerusalem, in return, enrich the givers by the communication of spiritual goods. It should come as no surprise, then, that the motif appears just as strongly in the personal interpretation Paul gives to his own apostolic activity (2 Cor 6:3-10).

The Apostle retraces his lot in seven antithetical formulas (6:8c-10), which conclude with these two pairs: "poor, yet we enrich many. We seem to have nothing, yet everything is ours" (6:10). In this "proud hymn of praise for his activity" (Lietzmann) and his faithfulness, Paul proceeds by repeated antitheses. Each time, the accent is on the positive side, which mentions the spiritual goods the missionary must supply in abundance. The negative formulas which preceed (e.g., "poor. . . .seem to have nothing") are only the negative complements which, for oratorical effect, should put the positive side in greater relief. Paul himself alludes to the passionate character of these affirmations: "Men of Corinth, we have spoken to you frankly, opening our hearts wide to you" (6:11). We must not push these formulas too hard, but must always keep in mind the literary form.

It seems, further, that in this enumeration the Apostle had recourse to certain schemas of the Stoic-Cynic diatribe.[25] The only formula which lies outside this type of schema is the remark that Paul "has enriched many." Certainly the Cynic philosopher, aware of being at the service of Zeus, as apostle and shepherd of men, could express himself in similar formulas. But with Paul they must be viewed against the backdrop of his apostolic mission and in the perspective of the history of salvation which is based on the mystery of Christ. In the same way that Christ made himself poor to enrich many, so too his Apsotle, who, by preaching and the sacrament, communicates to men the benefits of salvation in Jesus Christ, "in whom you have been richly endowed (by my preaching)" (1 Cor 1:5).

The concluding verse too, "having nothing, yet everything is ours," alludes to the goods of salvation. The one who possesses them is rich, even if he is poor according to the temporal order. Exterior poverty can exist and subsist perfectly well alongside spiritual riches, but it can no longer imprint the mark of poverty on human life. The riches of salvation offered by God in Jesus Christ dominate all the thought of Paul; he is fascinated by the riches of God and of Christ.

Because of this affirmation, the terms "poor" and "having nothing" (6:10) remain astonishingly imprecise and enigmatic. In regard to the riches of the work of salvation, the concrete circumstances of human life, whether riches or poverty, do not make any difference. Paul shows himself to be a Hellenist not only in his rhetoric but also in his fundamental attitude: when it comes to true happiness, to the true riches of man, the concrete circumstances of life merit no more than a passing mention.

Another example points in the same direction. The new order established by Christ abolishes all differences of nationality, sex, social conditions. "There does not exist among you Jew or Greek, slave or freeman, male or female" (Gal 3:28; Col 3:11). In each of these listings, "poor and rich" is lacking each time; this is quite typical of Paul's fundamental attitude.[26]

E. *The Problem of the Economic Condition of the Pauline Communities*

If we seek a justification for this peculiar phenomenon in the Pauline letters, perhaps this is the place to ask ourselves about the actual social situation of the communities.

1. In Paul's exhortations we do not find a single address to rich people, asking them to come to the aid of those who are economically weak. The idea of sustenance to be given to the needy appears, for the first time, in a very characteristic context, in Eph 4:28; "The man who has been stealing must steal no longer; rather, let him work with his hands at honest labor so that he will have something to share with those in need." We must immediately notice that the writer's focus is not at all on the needy but in honest work for the thief. An express invitation to help the needy, therefore, is lacking; thus the problem could not have been too urgent.

Still it goes without saying that, for Paul, fraternal communion includes the obligation of active charity and that the members of the same "body" (the same community) must take care of each other (1 Cor 12:26; see 11:18ff). However, the context shows that these remarks are not directed primarily to a manifestation of fraternal charity but rather to the fundamental idea of 1 Cor, that is, that there must not be divisions in a community. Consideration of the unity of the Church, which admits neither divisions nor rivalries, leads to the conclusion that it should not have needy people. Paul is the apostle of unity as much as fraternal charity.

2. We have no indication in the Pauline communities of any organized assistance for the poor, such as we find in the first community of Jerusalem (Acts 6). Still less do we find any attempt to organize a community of goods on the basis of Christian charity (see Acts 2:44, 4:32-37, 5:1-11). Likewise, we do not know what exact functions the "deacons" at Philippi exercised (Ph 1:1; Rom 12:7), nor those of "sister Phoebe", who was deaconness of the church of Cenchreae (Rom 16:1). We know only their titles, and from this we

might conclude (through wrongly) that these persons were given to "table service." But the fact is that we lack any indication of a practice in the Pauline churches analogous to that attested by Acts for Jerusalem. We do not even know if and up to what point the "supper of the Lord" served to help the poor (see 1 Cor 11:21). In every instance, Paul gives no particular attention to helping the poor.

3. The Jews of the Diaspora and their proselytes, to whom the preaching of Paul was adressed above all, were heads of businesses, commercial people, and well-off artisans. It is striking to note how Acts is at pains to present the most considerate and well-off members of the Pauline communities and to avoid giving the impression that the Christian communities were made up of the "modest" and poor.[27]

4. The letters of Paul confirm the impression given in Acts. "Macedonia supplied my needs" (2 Cor 11:8-9) while he was in Corinth; the Philippians had sent him gifts more than once to Thessalonica and later to Ephesus (Ph 4:16, 10). Even the community at Corinth, which we know the best, seems to have been, at least, a community of good bourgeoisie. When we examine, with this question in mind, the abuses noted and the problems posed in 1 Cor 1:1-17, we can see that they are proper to well-off situations. The collection itself is the best proof that the communities were not poor. In no place does Paul mention any indigence whatsoever. In 2 Cor 8:14 he calls to mind, even with a certain emphasis, their "plenty" and insists "that the relief of others ought not to impoverish you" (8:13) by gifts which are too generous. It is a question only of seeking a balance, an "equality."

We must conclude, therefore, against the widespread opinion which takes the allusion to "deep poverty" (2 Cor 8:2) in a very literal way, that the Pauline communities are to be ranked, according to our modern social scale, in the category of the well-off middle class. Since the problem of economic poverty was not posed in any urgent way, Paul does not give any precise theological presentation of poverty, such as developed in the Palestinian communities in line with the older biblical spirituality.

F. Beginnings of a Theology of Poverty not Exploited by Paul

1. *God Has Chosen What Is Weak.* The first indirect movement toward a theological clarification of the social condition of the community appears in 1 Cor 1:26-31. With his preference for paradoxical statements, Paul explains that the methods of God, viewed from a human perspective are only folly. A specific reference illustrates this affirmation: "Consider your situation. Not many of you are wise, as men account wisdom; not many are influential; and surely, not many are well-born. God chose those whom the world considers absured to shame the wise" (1 Cor 1:26-27). Behind this theology of election stands the biblical pattern of the elevation of the humble, a pattern which found diverse expressions in Palestinian spirituality. James also speaks of this election of the poor and weak (2:5) in terms that sound almost Pauline. But Paul does not develop this idea that God has chosen the "poor and the weak."[28] In fact, he wishes to sing the praises not of the poor and the economically weak but of the power of God in the "weakness" of the cross (1 Cor 1:18-30). And, what's more, it is likely that the situation of Corinth, to which he alludes, had no connection with the theme of the "elevation of the little people." There was in that community, if not "many" (according to Paul's phrase), at least a sufficient number of people who were highly regarded and influential in the view of the world.

2. *The Imitation of Christ.* Even the allusion to the

exemplary character of Christ's behavior, which Paul
used to justify the collection (2 Cor 8:9), does not lead
him to recommend an imitation of Christ in the sense
that the faithful should, like Jesus, make themselves
poor and consider voluntary poverty an ideal of life.
The point of comparison concerns only, as we have
seen, the positive aspect of the example: the Corinthians have a real possibility of "enriching many"
(2 Cor 6:10), in both the literal and figurative meanings of the word. The ideas of Hellenism and the
thought of Paul do not consider "making oneself poor"
a religious ideal to be followed. Even if we do not
take this into account, it is clear that what prevents
the Apostle from proclaiming an ideal of poverty as a
form of imitating the Lord is the particular manner
in which Christ made himself poor. According to 2
Cor 8:9, the "poverty" of Jesus is simply his human
existence, always bearing in itself the divine life. The
incarnation does not signify renunciation of divinity
but only the entrance into the weak human conditon:
"for your sake he made himself poor though he was
(and remained) rich" (2 Cor 8:9). This *kenōsis* could
not be imitated and therefore could not be proposed
as an example.

Based on the evidence we have, it seems that Paul
ignores the traditions of the Palestinian church on the
quality of discipleship that was reserved for those who
follow Jesus in his earthly ministry. But the decisive
reason for the absence of this theology of the *sequela
Christi* seems to be this: Pauline Christology and the
concrete conditions of the Christian life are determined
uniquely by the riches of the paschal Christ. Since
his conversion on the Damascus road, Paul had known
only this exalted Christ. This Christ, and his all-power-
ful presence, had changed the life of Paul and were
sufficient for him to complete the transformation of
his life.

3. *The Expectation of the Parousia.* It is frequently said
said that the ultimate reason why Paul does not mention the social conditions of his communities is this:
his expectation of the parousia (therefore a religious
motive) put all human preoccupations on a secondary
level. But this motif is not as convincing as one
imagines in the Pauline teaching—in fact, quite the
contrary.

As far as the organization of his communities is concerned, Paul starts from the general rule that each
one should remain in the state to which he or she has
been called. This rule applies not only to the condition of slaves but also to the problem of circumcision
(1 Cor 7:17-24), and it is decisive for the regulation
of marriages between members of different religions
(1 Cor 7:12-16). Although the problem is not raised
in the questions facing the Corinthians, we could add:
whether one is rich or poor, the only thing that counts
is to live in conformity with one's vocation, with the
call which changed the Christian's life by putting him
or her in relation to Christ. The specific conditions
in which one lives are unimportant.

The eschatological expectation of the parousia itself
is no reason to change one's state or condition in life.
Some Christians at Thessalonica, influenced no doubt
by the Apostle's teaching on the parousia, had dared
not to work but to live at the expense of the community. To these Paul addresses the principle: "Anyone who would not work should not eat" (2 Th 3:10).
With unusual sternness ("in the name of the Lord
Jesus Christ"), Paul commands them to dedicate themselves to honest work and so earn their living. The
community must reject members who squander themselves in a lazy and ill-regulated life. Even in 1 Th
(4:11-12) we find, alongside the warning to "admonish
the unruly," the warning, based on fraternal charity,
to "make it a point of honor to remain at peace and ·

attend to your own affairs. Work with your hands as
we directed you to do, so that you will give good example to outsiders and want for nothing.'' Christians
should not depend on anyone nor should they accept
outside help, but should give to all the example of
a work-filled life (see Col 4:5, etc.) For Paul, this is
a sign of fraternal love (see Eph 4:28).

On this point Paul himself is an eloquent example
for his communities: he always earned his own living
by the work of his hands.[29] This is so characteristic
of Paul that Acts, at the time of his farewell at
Miletus (20:34-35), presents it as a key trait of Paul:
''You yourselves know that these hands of mine have
served both my needs and those of my companions.
I have always pointed out to you that it is by such
hard work that you must help the weak (the poor).''[30]
In fact, from 2 Th 3:7-10 on, Paul explicitly presents
himself as an example to his communities on this
point. ''You know how you ought to imitate us. We
did not live lives of disorder when we were among
you, nor depend on anyone for food. Rather, we
worked day and night, laboring to the point of ex-
haustion so as not to impose on any of you. Not that
we had no claim on you, but that we might present
ourselves as an example for you to imitate. Indeed,
when we were with you we used to lay down this
rule that anyone who would not work should not
eat.''[31]

Paul is neither a utopian nor an idealist; he places
himself squarely on the solid terrain of reality. For
Paul, the expectation of the parousia changes the manner of life as little as the expectation of death would
distract a Stoic from the program of his day. Work
assures a sufficient income to the faithful, to whom
nothing was as repugnant as dependence on others,
To live off alms, even for religious motives, is incompatible with Paul's conception of life.

II. *Paul's Refusal to Be Supported by the Community*

Paul may have worked for his living but he preached the gospel without pay. We might see in him the first worker-priest. He presented himself as an example to his communities in caring for his own needs by hard work, but he never presents himself as an example for the free character of his preaching.[32] Paul considers this renunciation of support by the community an exception which concerns himself alone and which, because of his personal motivation, cannot be imitated.

A. *Renunciation to Avoid Compromising His Preaching*

Paul affirms in 1 Cor 9:12 that it is his own, personal decision to renounce community support so as not to place an obstacle to reception or preaching of the gospel. He notes that on the contrary, other preachers of the gospel, notably the apostles, the brothers of the Lord and Peter (9:5), do not observe the same practice as he himself and Barnabas (we have no teaching on the practice of Barnabas).[33] Because Paul does not find that their practice jeopardized their preaching, Paul's renunciation must be founded on the precarious missionary situation in which he found himself. He gives us a glimpse, in fact, of the suspicions the missionary preaching of the gospel was exposed to. In this milieu the itinerant preachers of Oriental divinities, of would-be wonderworkers and other charlatans, were disseminating their messages in a very self-serving way, and it was in relation to them that Paul wished to keep his distance. "The exhortation we deliver does not spring from deceit or impure motives or any sort of trickery . . . we were not guilty, as you well know, of flattering words of greed under any pretext, as God is our witness: Neither did we seek glory from men, you or any others" (1 Th 2:3, 5-6). Even though they are referred to only as

possibilities, Paul takes such reproaches to heart.³⁴ With
all his heart he fought against reproaches of this kind,
to guarantee that his preaching would be heard without human suspicions of this kind. (1 Th 2:10).

B. *His Own Justification of His Attitude: Paul Is the Slave of Christ*

1. *The Right of the Teacher and Apostle to Be Supported
by the Community.* Paul recognizes the right, especially
valid for a teacher, of being supported by his disciples.
"The man instructed in the word should share all he
has with his instructor" (Ga 6:6; 1 Tim 5:17; 1 Cor
9:7). All the other missionaries, except Paul and
Barnabas, lay claim to this right. Paul explicitly
defends it with the following arguments:

(a) It is a natural right. "Who plants a vineyard
and does not eat of its yield? What shepherd does not
nourish himself with the milk of his flock?" (1 Cor
9:7).

(b) It is a divine right of the Old Testament, based
on the Mosaic Law. "It is written in the law of
Moses, 'You shall not muzzle an ox when it is tread-
ing out grain'" (Dt 25:4; see 1 Tim 5:18). Following
principles of rabbinic exegesis, Paul explains that this
perscription concerns the preacher of the good news
(1 Cor 9:8-12). In this context Paul recalls that each
priest draws his sustenance from the revenues which
come from sacrifices. "Do you not realize that those
who work in the temple are supported by the temple?"
(1 Cor 9:13). And he finds this principle enunciated
in the Old Testament too (see Nm 18:8-31, Dt 18:
1-5).

(c) It is a divne right in the New Testament, based
on a positive disposition of the Lord. "Likewise the
Lord himself ordered that those who preach the gospel should live by the gospel" (1 Cor 9:14). Paul

repeats with persistence that provision given by the
Lord, found in Mt 10:10: "The workman, after all,
is worth his keep" and in Lk 10:7: "for the laborer
is worth his wage."[35] The Greek terms used here,
exousia, diatagma, dietaxen (1 Cor 9:14), and *misthos*
(Lk 10:7), show that Paul is not dealing with a mere
possibility but with a strict right of the preacher,
founded on the positive law of God (in the Old Testament) and of Jesus Christ (in the New Testament).[36]
This apostolic right is also firmly rooted in the awareness of the community: Paul's renunciation of community support was interpreted by some of them as
unequivocal proof that he was not an apostle and
therefore could not claim any apostolic privilege. In
the hands of his enemies, this represented a dangerous
weapon: his disinterestedness was exploited to ruin his
apotolic authority. Nevertheless, Paul refused to be
supported by the community. With his own kind of
pride he declares: "As for me I have not used any
of these rights . . . I would rather die than let anyone rob me of my boast" (1 Cor 9:15; 2 Cor 11:10).

2. *Justification of Paul's Attitude.* Paul gives the reason for his renunciation in 1 Cor 9:16-17: "Yet
preaching the gospel is not the subject of a boast;
I am under compulsion and have no choice. I am
ruined if I do not preach it! If I do it willingly, I
have my recompense (*misthos*); if unwillingly, I am
nonetheless entrusted with a charge." Paul feels that
he is living in a situation in which he owes obedience
as an attendant, a slave in the service of the Lord.

"What then is my recompense?" Paul does not answer the question. Everyone knows that an attendant
(a slave) receives his salary from the master of the
house if he faithfully accomplishes his task (see 1 Cor
4:1f), and that he receives no other pay from the
one to whom he renders the immediate service. Paul
considers his call to preach the gospel to be a "com-

pulsion, I have no choice"; he cannot hold himself
back. In effect, the call of Damascus had not been
the result of a free decision; he had been "seized"
by Christ (Ph 3:12), constrained, and conquered by
him as a victory trophy, a slave. Finding himself
in the service of Christ, he can preach his gosepl
only freely. "And this recompense of mine? It is simply this, that when preaching I offer the gospel free
of charge and do not make full use of the authority
the gospel gives me" (1 Cor 9:18).

Without any doubt whatsoever, Paul, as a preacher,
would have had the right to invoke the privilege of an
apostle to be supported by the community, but in his
particular case he could not; he is the slave of Christ.
But to guard against a misunderstanding which might
have arisen in the Greek milieu, he adds, "although
I am not bound to anyone I made myself the slave
of all" (1 Cor 9:19). He did this freely and his actions must be understood in a moral light. Paul realized
in his own life a *kenosis* in the service of Christ. He
considers his relationship with Christ so unique that it
cannot be imitated and is not obligatory for others.
He does not criticize the other apostles who act dif-
ferently from himself.

C. *Theological Clarification of Paul's Renunciation*

The theme of Paul's renunciation of his right to be
supported by the community plays a large role in the
two epistles which follow 1 Cor, that is, Philippians
and 2 Corinthians. Directly and indirectly, Paul seeks
to give his attitude a theological base.

In 1 Cor 9:19, Paul presented himself as a slave
of Christ and had defined his service as one of slavery:
"Although I am not bound to anyone, I made myself
the slave of all." To Greek ears, this voluntary *kenosis* would have sounded scandalous, and Paul's de-

tractors immediately confronted him with the remark
that he was acting just like a slave; they described
his mentality and attitude as *tapeinos*—low, servile, the
behavior of a slave. When he is at Corinth, they say,
he behaves like a weak, lowly man, but when he is
far from Corinth, he asserts himself boldly like a
strong man (2 Cor 10:1).

The appearance of these descriptions relating to
tapeinos, which occur only in Phil and 2 Cor, clearly
shows us how profoundly this reproach touched Paul, [37]
and on this matter he leaves us in no doubt. In connection with his renunication, the term appears again
in 2 Cor 11:7: "Could I have done wrong when I
preached the gospel of God to you free of charge,
humbling myself with a view to exalting you?" He had
"robbed" other churches, he adds, receiving support
from them (Philippi, Macedonia)'n order to serve the
Corinthians; but in Achaia he will not be deprived of
his title of glory. He wishes to be in debt to no one
(2 Cor 11:8-10).

1. When he says that he "made himself the slave
of all" (1 Cor 9:19), Paul takes up the words of his
detractors: they treat him as a lowly, vile man (2
Cor 10:1). But he takes this negative, pejorative description and, in the light of the "humbling-exalting"
theme dear to biblical, Palestinian spirituality, gives
it a new meaning. He turns it into a positive statement: he lowered himself in order to raise others up,
which means, in biblical language, to enrich others
by the preaching of the gospel. Outside the letter to
the Philippians, this theme appears only here, but with
a particular new meaning: Paul "lowers himself" so
that, in this way, he might "raise up" others. This
is what he has already said of himself, "poor, yet
we enrich many" (2 Cor 6:10) in the likeness of
Jesus who "made himself poor . . . so that you might
become rich" (2 Cor 8:9).

2. We will correctly understand this unusual expression in 2 Cor 11:7 only if we interpret it in light of the letter to the Philippians, which was probably written just a short time before at Ephesus. In Ph 4:10 ff, Paul describes his financial situation by recourse to the idea of *tapeinousthai* ("be brought low"), while denying that he lacks anything, as he is accustomed to living in most contradictory situations. He again expresses himself with oratorical antitheses: "I am experienced in being brought low (*tapeinousthai*), yet I know what it is to have an abundance (*perisseuein*) . . . I have learned how to eat well or go hungry, to be well provided for (*perisseuein*) or do without (*hystereisthai*)." In the last antithesis, the contrary of *perisseuein* is no longer *tapeinousthai*, as in the first, but *hystereisthai*. Paul therefore understands *tapeinousthai* in the sense of a precarious life, the privation of external goods. Applied to the specific situation, the statement has the meaning "to know how to live without financial assistance." Faced with living conditions ranging from one extreme to the other, Paul had learned how to do this.

In verse 11 the antithesis is preceded by a statement which provides a new key to understanding Paul's renunciation: "for whatever the situation I find myself in I have learned to be self-sufficient." The *autarkeia* claimed by Paul does not mean, in the first instance, a materially sober life but the fundamental virtue of Stoic philosophy, interior detachment in relation to exterior goods. Paul continues to affirm his independence even vis-à-vis the Philippians. He is not an employee of the community, who might receive a salary from it; he is free, and wishes to safeguard his freedom in relation to the contributions of the Philippians. His independence is something precious for him, which is as much threatened by poverty as by riches.[38]

But in spite of his recourse to Stoic terminology, the *autarkeia* of Paul is characterized by his close union with the Lord. He is able to attain *autarkeia* not by an act of personal virtue but by the strength of Christ: "In him who is the source of my strength, I have strength for everything" (Ph 4:13). Only complete communion with Christ permits Paul to be self-sufficient in every situation; it assures him the "distance" from the goods of this world which he needs to accomplish his mission. [39]

3. It is surely no accident that Paul returns still again to the idea of *tapeinos*, apropos of another passage of the letter to the Philippians. He strongly exhorts the Philippians (2:1-11) to *tapeinophrosynē*, to "modesty of feeling," to have the mentality of a *tapeinos*, and thus realize "unanimity" and not give way to arguments in the community (perhaps an allusion to the situation at Corinth?)

He justifies this exhortation by referring to the example of Jesus Christ. The hymn to Christ which Paul inserts in verses 5-11 sketches the way of salvation followed by Christ. Moreover, in conformity with Paul's way of thinking, the way of Christ toward *kenōsis* is exploited (2:6-8). "Though he was in the form of God, he did not deem equality with God something to be grasped at. Rather he emptied himself and took the form of a slave, being born in the likeness of men . . . and it was thus that he humbled himself, obediently accepting even death, death on a cross" Once more Paul presents his Greek readers, enamored of the idea of liberty, with the idea of making oneself a slave. At the center of this motivation, between affirming that Jesus "took the form of a slave (*morphē doulou*)" (2:7) and that "he made himself obedient" (2:8b), Paul uses the phrase *etapeinōsen heauton,* which, in view of verse 9 ("because of this God highly exalted him"), we usually translate "he humbled himself" (Vulgate:

humiliavit seipsum).

Perhaps we could resolve a difficulty relating to the structure of this hymn[40] if we interpret this incidental remark in a Hellenistic sense and not take account of the biblical theme of the spirituality of the poor with its antithesis, "humbling-exalting." "He took the condition of a slave." Here too Paul takes up the slogan of his Corinthian detractors (2 Cor 10:1), who treated him as lowly, as *tapeinos*. This interpretation finds support in the fact that Paul uses in Phil (2:8a, 9) the same terms he uses of himself in 2 Cor (11:7): "humbling myself with a view to exalting you." This profession of personal faith, which does not derive from the biblical spirituality of the poor, appears for the first time in 1 Cor 9:19: "Although I am not bound to anyone, I made myself the slave of all." Thus in two instances the idea of *kenōsis* appears in relation to the question of pay (1 Cor 9:19; 2 Cor 11:7) and once (between 1 and 2 Cor) in the letter to the Philippians (2:7).

If we are correct in bringing together the critics in Corinth and the thesis developed in Ph 2, we have an indication—delicate but clear—of the Christological basis of Paul's refusal to depend on his communities. As the slave of Christ, Paul imitates his example: he takes the condition of slave for the love of Jesus (2 Cor 4:5) and for the service of the community. As the slave of Christ, he cannot dare to receive a salary for services rendered. His mission is to carry out what the Lord orders him to do, and it is from the Lord that he receives his salary. This understanding that Paul has of himself and his role is no doubt unique in the history of the primitive Church. In the discussion of the renunciation of support from the churches, we do not know if, or how far, Paul exploited this motif of imitating the attitude of Christ, who "took the form of a slave" for us (Ph 2:7). In con-

formity with this last passage, Paul's theological justification of his attitude is only begun. This much is
certain: Paul considered his disinterestedness a personal privilege, his own title to boast, and on this
point he presented himself as an example to no one.

III. Conclusions

We can now sum up the results of our inquiry in
seven points:

1. Since the problem of social poverty was not a
real one in the Pauline communities, we do not find
this theme developed in the epistles. When Paul uses
the term "poor" and applies it to himself or to Christ,
it is always in relation to the opposite terms "rich"
or "enrich" where his primary emphasis lies (2 Cor
6:10, 8:1ff). In Ga 2:10 and Rom 15:26, Paul mentions, a propos of the collection, the "poor" in Jerusalem, but here he is citing from their own description
of themselves. We can say, therefore, that the term
"poor" is absent from Pauline vocabulary.

2. The call to faith enables us to discover "in
Christ" a new dimension of salvation, which does
not change the specific, earthly conditions of life for
the Christian. Each Christian realizes "in his own
state" the demands of the economy of salvation, whose
riches rule the faithful in Christ. In relation to it,
exterior conditions of life are not essential (see 1 Cor
7:17-24). Paul does not know a particular way of
following Christ, such as the synoptics propose.

3. As for the goods of this world, which have no
lasting value, the Christian must live in *autarkeia*.
This spiritual distancing and independence from exterior goods belongs to Christian spirituality (1 Tim
6:6; Ph 4:11); it is not for Paul a human achieve-
ment, as in Stoic philosophy, but a charism. "In him
who is the source of my strength I have strength for

everything" (Ph 4:13).

4. Paul demands that every Christian provide for his needs by proper and serious work (1 Th 4:12; 2 Th 3:10; Acts 20:34f). Even religious considerations, such as the expectation of the parousia, do not dispense from this obligation. Paul does not know a voluntary poverty. We must never forget that, according to the social order of the ancient world, everyone who worked belonged to the class of the "not-rich," that is, was one of the "poor."

5. Paul's refusal to be supported by the community is a consquence of his personal relationship with Christ, resulting from the occurrence on the road to Damascus. Paul is the slave of Christ; he proclaims the gospel at Christ's order and, consequently, receives his payment only from Christ. But the fundamental right of the preacher and teacher to receive what he needs from his disciples is explicitly recognized and confirmed by Paul (1 Cor 9:4-17; Gal 6:6).

6. It is possible to discern the beginnings of a Christological justification of Paul's voluntary stripping of himself in his attempts to connect it with the exemplary self-emptying of Christ (Ph 2:5-11) in the direction of *tapeinos* (2 Cor 10:1, 11:7; Ph 4:12). Pauline theology includes many elements that are susceptible of further development but have not been exploited by the Apostle. Both the commentary on the collection (2 Cor 8-9) and the discussion of personal disappropriation (Ph 2:5-11) refer to the example of Christ. However, it is not the example of his earthly life which made an impression on Paul but rather the basic event of salvation itself, presented each time as a *kenōsis*. According to Paul, this *kenōsis* can be imitated only in virtue of an accidental relationship: Christ made himself a slave. For the love of Christ, a free man can make himself a slave for others (Ph 2:5-11). There is no question here of a substantial relation-

ship to Christ, who "being rich made himself poor," that is, became man in the incarnation (2 Cor 8:9).

7. The influence of the Palestinian spirituality of poverty on the thought of Paul is minimal and reflects only the theme of "humbling-exalting" (1 Cor 1:18ff., "God chose that which is weak;" 2 Cor 11:7; Ph 2:5-11). Such forms of spirituality were strange to the Greek world. Even the particular Palestinian traditions concerning Jesus (e.g., the synoptic traditions) are unkown to Paul.

Paul sought, and discovered, a proper way to define the Christian life and to resolve its problems. The norms of his morality flow from the paschal condition of the Christian who has become, "in Jesus Christ," a new creature (Gal 3:27; Col 3:11). And from the paschal reality of Christ he draws consequences which determine the Christian's paschal life. In relation to the "riches of Christ", all earthly realities have, to a certain degree, simply ceased to exist.

Footnotes

1. Poverty and indigence are a "training ground for virtue" (Arkesilaos to Stobeus, *Ecl* 5, 784:13-16). The Stoics regularly conducted themselves according to the maxim "whoever is free of property is also free of cares." When life is no longer worth living because of exterior poverty or other reasons, one is able to leave this life with dignity and freedom.

2. On this subject, see the study of A. George above. According to the reports of Josephus and Philo, the Essenes practiced community of goods and lived a sober, simple life. But the manuscripts from Qumran are not all that explicit.

They say that one's previous fortune, up to then considered profane, can contribute to the holiness of the community (1 QS 1:12 and elsewhere), but they make no mention of any common use of things nor of personal poverty, although in their hymns these "pious" frequently call themselves "the poor." They live in exile as "the poor of Yahweh", persecuted by their religious adversaries.

3. The saying of Jesus to the rich young man is reported in all three synoptic gospels (Mk 10:17-31, etc.), as well as the remark of Peter: "We have left all things and followed you" (Mk 10:28, etc). Matthew's phrase (10:37f.) "Whoever loves his father more than me is not worthy of me" is modified by Luke (14:26) in the sense of a demand imposed on those who follow Jesus. On the meaning of the pericope of the call of the rich man, see the study of S. Légasse above.

4. Bibliography on Pauline and Johannine theology is abundant but here we will mention only two: J. Fitzmyer, "Pauline Theology," *JBC*, no. 79, and B. Vawter, "Johannine Theology," *JBC*, No. 80.

5. With the exception of Paul's central teaching on the death of Jesus (the theology of the cross), teaching on the earthly Jesus is minimal (1 Thes 4:15; 1 Cor 7:10; see also 7:25, 9:14, 11:23).

6. A. Schulz, *Nachfolgen und Nachahmen* (Munich: Kosel, 1962) pp. 270-288.

7. Cited in B. Rigaux, *The Letters of St. Paul* (Chicago: Franciscan Hearld Press, 1968) pp 107-108. On 1 Tim 6:16-19, see fn. 39 below.

8. The term is found especially in 2 Cor 9:9 in a citation from the LXX (Ps 111 (112):9) in the midst of the discussion on the collection. It is a proper characteristic of the pious person to show mercy to the poor ("Lavishly he gives to the poor"). The Greek *penēs* (one who earns his living by hard work) does not evoke the idea of the need for charitable assistance; the LXX transforms the piety of the poor as it appears in the Old Testament. If Paul cites the psalm verse, it is not because he is dealing with questions of "the poor" but because the psalm provides an example of magnanimous generosity.

9. See the quotation from Plutarch 553 (Aristophanes) cited under the entry *penēs* in W. Bauer, *A Greek-English Lexicon of*

the New Testament, trans. W. F. Arndt and F. W. Gingrich (Chicago: University of Chicago Press, 1957) p. 648.*

10. On these Greek terms see F. Hauck, *"Penēs,"* TDNT, 6:37-40, and F. Hauck and E. Bammel, *"Ptōchos,"* TDNT, 6:885-915.

11. This is an honorific title, applied especially to Judeo-Christian communities as communities of eschatological salvation. 1 Cor 16:15 tells us that the house of Stephanas at Corinth was devoted to the "service of the saints." (See Rom 15:25, 31: 2 Cor 8:4). Was he perhaps the organizer of the collection at Corinth?

12. On dating the redaction of the epistle to the Galatians a bit prior to Romans (at Corinth, winter 57/58), see P. Seidensticker, *Paulus. Der verfolgte Apostel Jesu Christi* (Stuttgarter Bibelstudien) (Stuttgart: V. Katholisches Biblewerk, 1965), 8:68ff.

13. The collection of Acts 11:27-30 was a one-time operation, prόvoked by the catastrophic famine of A.D. 45 under the emperor Claudius and the procurators Fadus and Tiberius Alexandrus.

14. This is the opinion of M. J. Lagrange in his *St. Paul: Epitre aux Galates* (Paris: J. Gabalda, 1950), ad. loc. In the Jerusalem Bible, S. Lyonnet translates Rom 15:26, "for the needs of the saints of Jerusalem who are in poverty." See also the commentaries of O. Kuss, Fr. Althaus, J. Kürzinger, and T. Zahn.*

15. See the commentaries of O. Michel, H. Lietzmann, H. W. Beyer, H. Schlier, and E. Bammel (*TDNT,* 6:909).*

16. Bammel, *TDNT,* 6:909: "The saints" (partitive genitive) can also designate the assembly of the community of Israel within which are found "the poor," i.e., the community of salvation. (In this case, "the poor" would not be the only expression to designate Jerusalem.) But it is certainly preferable to interpret the genitive in the interpretive or corrective sense: "the poor"—i.e., "the saints of Jerusalem." In this case the two titles designate the community of Jerusalem.

17. Following Bammel (*TDNT,* 6:909, fn. 224), the passages in 2, 9cd, and 10a (they "gave Barnabas and me the handclasp of fellowship, signifying that we should go to the Gentiles and they to the Jews. The only stipulation was that we should be mindful of the poor.") are taken from the "minutes" (*procès-verbaux*). Gal 2:7-9b would then be the Pauline interpretation

of the decision. But verses 7 and 8 must likewise be considered part of the "minutes"; only here do we find (and twice!) the Greek title "Petros" (7b and 8a), whereas Paul always inserts "Kephas" in the context, (9a, 11, and elsewhere).

18. Lagrange, *Gal:* "This 'remembrance of the poor is a delicate way of expressing the collection of alms."

19. O. Michel, "*Mimnēskomai*," *TDNT,* 4:675-683.

20. The western reading of Rom 12:13, "Look on the needs of the saints as your own. Be generous in offering hospitality," is ably and convincingly defended by T. Zahn, as reviewed by F . Hauck in *TDNT,* 6:37-40. The usual reading is "Take part in the needs of the saints." See the context.

21. Cited following O. Kuss in *II. Kor* (Regensburg: F. Pustet, 1940).

22. Paul expressly calls it a "tie of unity," a *koinōnia* (Rom 15:26f). On the question of what the collection means in the life and activity of an independent missionary in Ephesus, see my *Paulus,* pp. 54ff.

23. See 1 Cor 16:17; Phil 2:30; Col 1:24.

24. Paul often speaks in this way of the fullness of the riches of the goodness of God (Rom 2:4), of the riches of his glory (Rom 9:23), of the "depth of the riches" (cf. the depths of poverty, 2 Cor 8:2) of the wisdom and of the knowledge of God (Rom 11:33), etc.

25. Windisch, "The rhetoric is that of the diatribe; certain antithetical formulas are probably of Hellenistic origin." Analogies can be found, e.g., in Epictetus, *Diss II,* 19, 24; Philo, *Omn. Prob Lib. 77,* "in need, but very rich." [a]

26. For an opposite usage see Rv 13:16, "It (the beast) forced all men small and great, rich and poor, slave and free, to accept a stamped image on their right hand or their forehead." In the rabbinic literature, the antinomy "rich and poor" is mentioned only once (*Ex Rab* 21:83c): "In the name of R. Eliezar (*ca.* A.D. 270), men make a distinction between the rich and the poor, but not God; before him, all are the same: women and slaves, poor and rich." Later rabbis know only the enumeration "pagan or Israelite, man or woman, domestic or servant" (three times in *Seder Elijjahu Rabba, Midrash,* from tenth century A.D.).

27. Acts 16:14; Lydia, a dealer in purple goods from the town of

Thyatira at Phillippi; 17:4-9: "numerous prominent women," and
Jason, among others, at Thessalonica; 17:12: "numerous influential
Greek men and women" at Beroea; 17:34: "Dionysius, a member
of the court of the Areopagus, a woman named Damarus and a
few others " at Athens; 18:7-8: Titus Justus, Crispus, the head
of the synagogue at Corinth; 1 Cor 1:14, 16: Crispus, Gaius,
Stephanas; 1:11: Chloe; Rom 16:23-24: Gaius, Erastus, the city
treasurer. The identification of this last person with the edile Erastus, mentioned in an inscription for paving the streets of Corinth
at his own expense, remains problematic.

28. The idea that the poor might be considered religiously and
morally closer to God is unkown among the Greeks. In social
conflicts, they "could not even invoke the help of the gods"
(F. Hauck, *TDNT*, 6:886-887)."

29. At Corinth, Paul worked as a tent-maker for Aquila (and Pris-
cil) (Acts 18:1-3). Since Aquila was also with Paul at Ephesus, we
can admit that he gave him a job there too (Acts 18:18; I Cor
16:19; the western texts add "with whom I found hospitality").
During his captivity, when Paul was not able to provide for his
needs from his own work, he gladly received help from the Philippians (4:10-20). He needed assistance in the same way during his
stay at Corinth.

30. This idea of Luke is absent in Paul (see Eph 4:28).

31. This maxim certainly comes from either Greek or Jewish
proverbial wisdom, but up till now this has not been verified.

32. His practice corresponds to the rabbinic custom of having a
job as well as instructing students without charge. But this practice is contested. Thus Sir 38:24-34 stresses the incompatibility
between the study of Scripture and a manual occupation. Paul
also admits the practice of receiving a salary for instruction given
(Gal 6:6; 1 Cor 9:4-14).

33. According to Acts 4:36, Barnabas sold some land and placed
the proceeds at the disposition of the apostles in order to help
the needy. We can ask if the renunciation of support from the
community is related to this similarly charitable attitude? Or did
Barnabas remain a man of means even after the sale of the land?

34. See the commentaries. Paul several times mentions the
reproach leveled against him of being eager for gain (Phil 4:17;
2 Cor 11:7ff 12:13-18). In the same way, Paul defends himself
(Gal 1:10) against the charge of trying to gain human approval.

35. The addition in Mt 10:8, "The gift you have received, give

as a gift", contradicts Mt. 10:10 and is lacking in Mark and Luke. The renunciation of purse, bread, and money (see the context), mentioned in the missionary commission of the apostles, is expressly picked up again by Jesus in his farewell discourse (Lk 22:35f). The missionary situation after the resurrection demands that missionaries be equipped for every necessity (purse, traveling bag, sword).

36. W. Foerster (*"Exousia," TDNT,* 2:562): *misthos* designates the wages that can be demanded for a work accomplished.

37. Grundmann (*"Tapeinos," TDNT,* 8:18, fn. 48) is aware of this relation between Phil and 2 Cor. We would also note that the title "slave of Christ", which Paul gives himself, appears for the first time in 1 Cor 9:19 ("I made myself the slave of all") and again in 2 Cor 4:5 ("ourselves as your servants for Jesus' sake"). It is not found anywhere elese in the two letters to the Corinthians (taking the polemic into account), but appears once in Phil 1:1, where Timothy is also mentioned. Here its meaning is more attenuated, interpreted in the light of *tapeinophrosynē* ("to have humble, modest sentiments" (Phil 2:1ff, 4:12). Only the letters to the Galatians (1:10) and the Romans (1:1), both written near the end of Paul's stay in Corinth (winter 57/58), use the expression in a self-explanatory way. We might ask if the tensions at Corinth, dealing with Paul's self-understanding, have been left behind?

38. From the lexical point of view, see G. Kittel, *"Autarkeia," TDNT* 1:466-467.

39. According to 1 Tim 6:6, *autarkeia* is also an essential element in Christian spirituality. The behavior of itinerant preachers, who were very anxious to be paid for their teaching and inclined to "value religion only as a means of personal gain," inspires this response from the author: "There is of course great gain in religion—provided one is content with a sufficiency"; that is, provided it is joined to *autarkeia.* Here too we are dealing with the Stoic idea of freedom in relation to ties of this world. From this fundamental attitude arise sobriety and disinterestedness. The author of this letter uses other motifs of the Stoic-Cynic diatribe in his argumentation (6:7-10). On the ther hand, the Palestinian parenesis is found in the exhortation to the rich "to be generous, sharing what you have" (6:17-19). They should put their hope not in perishable goods but in God and their good works (Mt 6:20; Lk 12:21).

40. The hymn in Phil 2:5-11 (following the schema "humbling-

exalting'') is composed of a formula of self-emptying (6-8), *kenōsis,* and a strophe on exaltation (9-11). It is more the idea of *kenōsis* (rather than incarnation) which we find in 2 Cor 8:9 (see 1 Cor 9:19); in Jn 13:3ff. (see Jn 1:18); in the letter of the community of Lyon to the communities of Asia Minor (Eusebius, *Eccl. Hist.,* 5:2,2); and in Heb 5:7-10, 12:2-3 (which alludes to the exalting). The hymn deals in the present with Christ's divine prerogatives, which certainly carried and undergirded the historical work of salvation and rendered it fruitful (aorist), but whose full use the God-made-man freely renounces (''he emptied himself'' (2:7). What seems out of place are the two lines on the man Jesus Christ between the lines "slave" and "obedient". This seems, in fact, to be the least natural place for the expression "he emptied himself." The strophe on *kenōsis* gains a certain unity if we see in the two lines on "man" an interjection (acclamation of the community?) as a refrain (Pliny, *Letters,* 10, 96-97) and if we understand the line on abasement in one of the following ways: (1) it is extracted by Paul from the strope on the exaltation and clarified by the context in the meaning of "become a slave" or (2) it is a Pauline addition in response to the reproaches of the Corinthians (2 Cor 10:1, 11:7).

The Radicalism of the Kingdom

Beda Rigaux O.F.M.

As we conclude this colloquim on the biblical teachings concerning the poor and poverty, we find that our endeavor has proved rich in results.[1] The place of the poor appears privileged in the biblical message, both at the point of departure (the Old Testament) and at the point of arrival (the New Testament). On the one hand, the poor person is an object of special divine favor and of the religious obligations of justice and charity on the part of believers. On the other hand, poverty represents an opening to the call of the Messiah; an opening to liberty and to God's total gift by renunciation, that fundamental disponability which links the disciple to the person and work of the Messiah; an opening to the heroic exercise of *agapē* of which the life of the primitive community in Jerusalem presents the clearest image.

Nevertheless, the newness of the teaching on the poor and poverty in the Christian economy consists in the union of the disciple with the person of the teacher and the gospel which he preaches and incarnates. The complete change of life which the condition and consequence of the good news implies is a life where riches and the goods of this world have no value in and for themselves. Material despoilment, the poverty of the Messiah, was soon interpreted as an image of the abasement of him who "made himself poor . . . so that you might become rich" (2 Cor 8:9), who "though he was in the form of God . . . emptied himself and took the form of a slave" (Ph 2:6-7) in order "to bring glad tidings to the poor" (Lk 4:18). The authors of the New Testament, heirs and heralds of the Church-in-formation, were well aware of these different aspects of the gospel. The more we examine the sacred texts, the more these revealed realities appear in their truth and fruitfulness.

After the four preceding papers have done their work, our task would seem to be over. The essentials have been said, and, I hasten to add, said by excellent specialists with great clarity. But at the risk of repeating some themes already studied, it seemed useful to clarify the statements on the poor and poverty by trying to grasp the very event which brought the teachings to such serious expression, where paradox and polemic forge the harsh formulas, marking the teaching and call of the gospel with gravity, seriousness, even tragedy. But we would like to make it clear at the outset that the radicalism does not seem to us to be limited to the mere formulas, nor was it due only to the pedagogical or polemical needs of the preaching of Jesus.

It might have been useful, were it possible, to set the radicalism of Jesus within the framework of his times. The Hasidim (the Pious) of the Maccabean period gave rise to various movements: on the one hand the Pharisees and on the other the Essenes of Qumran, whose radicalizing reinterpretation of the Law transformed its more ancient observance. The first-century Zealots, a branch of Phariseeism, combined violent means of resistance against the occupying power (Rome) and a doctrine of God, the only Lord, and his coming final victory. Jesus' hearers were living in a time when political conditions as well as religious practices demanded a religious attitude marked by an acute exigency.

Our effort here, imperfect and partial as it might be, will deal with material in the synoptic gospels. Without being able in each instance to distinguish between the words of Jesus and their use by the redactors of the gospels, we shall try to reach the most ancient layer of the tradition. On this level the originality and the novelty of the message take on their most solid density. We are helped here by a very large agreement among exegetes, at least among those exegetes who do not consider all the texts to be creations of the community.

We must admit a last limitation: we must choose among the radicalizing words of Jesus. We have tried to keep to those which seemed to us the most closely related to gospel detachment. But since the radicalism of Jesus in relation to the goods of this world and the poor cannot be separated from his teaching on the relationship between the teacher and the disciple, it is only after establishing the literary and real substructure of the teacher-disciple relationship that we will be able to reset the detachment and interior arming of the disciple within the living context of the preaching of Jesus. This is why we will look first at the meaning of discipleship and only then at the renunciations it demands.

I. To Follow Jesus

Jesus was neither a solitary thinker nor a teacher of wisdom, nor an ascetic, nor a mystic retired from the world. His public activity was marked by an itinerant preaching career. The gospels unanimously put him in contact with the crowds which swarmed around him, pursuing him so that he could scarcely save himself from them. The same evangelists, and Mark in particular, give us to understand that his hearers glorified the "power" of his teaching and that the crowds sought the benefits of his wonder-working strength. It was from this audience that Jesus chose and attached a group of adherents to his person and his teaching. He made disciples.

This phenomenon is important and deserves our attentive consideration. The Jew knew the institution of rabbis and their disciples; John the Baptist, for instance, had his disciples. We want to underline the difference, the originality, even the uniqueness of the disciples of Jesus.

A. Jesus Was Not a Rabbi

The Jewish doctors taught the Law and the interpretation of the Law. At the time of Jesus they were divided into two rival schools, one going back to Hillel and the other to Shammai. The rabbi taught in a fixed place, surrounded by his disciples, his students, who were made up of men only; his authority derived only from his proper exegesis of the Law and the traditions of the "fathers," which enjoyed an authority as great as the sacred text itself. The rabbi could be both a witness and a preacher of the messianic expectation, but under the form of a general expectation of the eschatological act of God.

As Mark and Matthew report, Jesus was addressed by the title "rabbi" (Mk 9:5, 11:21, 14:45) or *rab-*

boni (10:51). This title does not place Jesus in the class of Jewish doctors; it can be only an honorific title for someone who teaches (Mt 23:8). Originally, "rabbi" meant only "mister." On the other hand, if Jesus did in fact teach, if he composed artistic parables and aphorisms, if he taught in the synagogues, if he gathered students around himself, if he argued with his enemies, and if he had recourse to the Law with astonishing assurance, we can see that he and the rabbis shared certain traits in common. But even taking all of them together, we cannot conclude to an identity of function between them.

Jesus' originality consisted in the connection between his teaching and the authority of his person. The I-say-to-you's are significant. Even when he refers to the Law, the Law does not have the last word for this new prophet. We must note, further, his preaching on the coming kingdom: his eschatology detaches him from the scholarly functions. His moral message too must be interpreted by the function of the end which is coming and which is already here. M. Hengel has summed up the New Testament data well: "Between him (Jesus) and the rabbis, there is not a difference of degree as between two teachers, but a difference of principle. He taught as one who had received from God, in an exceptional way, full powers to such an extent that his word was the word of God, and men were not able to remove themselves from it" (p. 55).

Equally expressive is the image of the disciple. He is not a *talmid*, the disciple of the Pharisees. The synoptics used two words to situate the disciples; they come "to follow" Jesus or "to accompany" him.[2] The disciple of the Pharisee also "follows" his master. He admires him, is proud of his condition, obeys and accepts his teaching. In every instance, "to follow" means to a good, docile student, one who is able to remember the teaching. The disciple is like Hanina ben Doxa, who came to Galilee and to Rabbi ben Zakkai "to study the Torah." K. H. Rengstorf, whose knowledge of the rabbinic writings is excellent, sees in rabbinism a strong intellectualizing movement within Jewish piety, based on the Old Testament. *Halaka*, the way of the master, became the norm for the disciple's conduct. One shared in the manner of life of the school; one helped in the elaboration of doctrines; one benefited from the techniques of memorization.

When the apprentice years were over, one became an important rabbi in turn as did, Rabbi Akiba. "At age 40 he retired to study the Torah; after 13 years, he taught Torah to a large number" (cf. Hengel, p. 59). After their period of formation, when they had assiduously learned their subject matter, the rabbis settled in a particular place. At this time the institution could still be connected with the various religious movements of the period, especially with Phariseeism and even with Zeiotism. Although they were teachers, rabbis were also witnesses and participants in prophetic and eschatological movements. The catastrophes of A.D. 70 and 135 marked the end of this function of rabbinism. The Pharisaic party of Shammai disappeared, and all activity became a school affair.

B. *The Call of Disciples*

The disciple of Jesus joined the master's company only when he had been called, that is, by vocation. The candidate does not decide for himself. We have some examples (representing only types) of those vocations in the calls of Jesus. For Simon and Andrew, "Come after me (*Deute opisō mou)*"; for James and John, "he called them (*ekalesen autous)*"; for Levi, "follow me (*akalouthei moi)*"; for the seventy-two disciples, "he chose them (*anedeixen*)"³ Mark explicitly uses and amplifies this theology of the call in the account of the choosing of the twelve: "he summoned the men he himself had decided upon (*proskaleitai hous ethelen autos*)." The emphatic use of *autos* is significant.

The one who is called does not then become a student of the Law, nor does he aspire to become a master, a rabbi. In fact, he will be explicitly forbidden to let himself be called "rabbi." His state is to *follow Jesus*, which means, above all, to have heard the good news of God. "This is the time of fulfillment. The reign of God is at hand!" (Mk 1:15). He clings to it by faith and is immediately associated with the itinerant life of Jesus. But before his commitment, he must think. When a scribe approached Jesus and said to him, "Teacher, wherever you go, I will come after you", Jesus said to him: "The foxes have lairs, the birds in the sky have nests, but the Son of Man has nowhere to lay his head" (Q; Mt 8:19-20; Lk 9:57-59). The parables of building a tower and of the king preparing to go to war offer two examples of the prudence and calculation which are necessary before making a commitment (Lk 14:28-33). And the disciple recognizes the absolute sovereignty of Jesus. It is God who acts through him. The power of God is the power of Jesus in the word and actions which work miracles.

Once he is committed, the disciple participates in the activity of Jesus. He is found in Jesus' company and is called *mathētēs*, a technical term which defines the group. It occurs 46 times in Mark; Luke uses it 37 times, but Matthew, by contrast, uses it 73 times. Of 671 verses in Mark, 498 (about 76 percent of the gospel) tell of words or actions of Jesus where the disciples are present. None of the other synoptics matches this proportion. Matthew and Luke do not mention them in passages where they are present in

Mark. It is very difficult, if not impossible, to determine in most of the incidents if it is the twelve we are
dealing with or a larger group. Mark distinguishes
carefully between the disciples and the crowd.[4] Adhering to Jesus according to Mark, is situated in a
movement where the unity between the prophet of
Nazareth and the hearer of his word is constantly
assured.

C. Education of the Disciples

In this closeness with Jesus, the disciple's faith receives an education. "Everything is possible to a man
who trusts" (Mk 9:23). In a hyperbolic turn of
phrase, Jesus said in another place, "Put your trust
in God. I solemnly assure you, whoever says to this
mountain, 'Be lifted up and thrown into the sea,'
and has no inner doubts but believes that what he
says will happen, shall have it done for him" (Mk
11:22-23). Faith saves (Mk 2:5) and heals (Mk 2:5,
9:23-24). The disciple must learn to act no longer
because of a commandment of the Torah but "because you belong to Christ" (Mk 9:41).

With faith, the disciple enters into an understanding of the coming of the kingdom. Mark, more than
the others, makes a point of the difficult time Jesus
had in making himself understood. The disciples do not
understand the parables (Mk 4:13). They still do not
have faith after the storm was stilled (Mk 4:40; cf.
Mt 8:26; Lk 8:25). They did not get the point of the
miracle of the multiplication of the loaves (Mk 6:52,
8:17-21; Mt 16:18-21). They are without understanding (Mk 7:18; Mt 15:16-17). We must not rest content with hearing and seeing. Faith leads to understanding that Jesus is the instrument of the victory of
God. It is, in the last analysis, a gift of God and of
Jesus, who "has done everything well. He makes the

deaf hear and the mute speak" (Mk 7:37).

Faith and understanding place the disciple, according
cording to the often repeated phrases "with Jesus,"
and this being "with Jesus" marks association with the
drama of Jesus.[5] Sealed by faith and enriched by a
special understanding, a true community formed the
immediate entourage of Jesus and associated the disciple with his mission and fate. Within this group,
a distinct place was set aside for the twelve. As Mark
notes explicitly, Jesus called them *hina ōsin met'autou*,
so that they might be with him.

D. Particular Instructions

After leaving Galiee, the master reserved to the
twelve and to the most faithful disciples some particular instructions. They had recognized in him the
Messiah (Mk 8:27-30; Mt 16:13-20; Lk 9:18-21);
they had begun to accustom themselves to the idea of
his death (Mk 9:31); they had gone up with him to
Jerusalem, the place where Jesus, like any prophet
must die (Lk 13:33). Mark reserves to them the eschatological discourse (Mk 13) and other instructions
(Mk 9:9-13, 33-50, 10:13-16, 23-31, 35-45). Matthew adds to this picture. The fourth great discourse
is addressed to them (18:1-35), as well as other instructions (19:1-12, 16-26, 27-30, 20:1-16, 20-23,
24-28). Luke wishes to prepare the disciples in view
of the "exodus" to come (Lk 9:22, 31, 34). The disciples benefit from numerous bits of advice throughout
the "journey" which are proper to them (Lk 9:51-
19:28). While this section of the gospel tells of only
three miracles (13:10-17, 14:1-6, 17:11-19), teaching
and instruction abound. We find material on the person of the disciple and his vocation (9:57-62), his
mission (10:1-20), the messianic revelation (10:21-24),
the providence which is specially reserved for them

(11:1-13), almsgiving (12:13-34), life in community (17:1-6), and messianic and eschatological expectation (12:35-53, 17:20-37). Further, this section of Luke contains no less than 24 parables, the unique riches of the book.

If the three evangelists trace a picture for us whose fundamental traits are shared by all, each of them nonetheless touches up the portrait in his own particular way. Mark is closest to the event, to the lack of understanding of the disciples, to familiarity with Jesus. Human traits of the master abound; the disciples are all caught up in his tragedy. Luke has detached the disciple from Jesus to accord to the Messiah his preeminence as Lord and head (*epistatēs*); the Messiah is already clothed with great majesty. In Matthew, Jesus, the new master of a new justice, instructs the Church of the evangelist's own time, explaining the mystery, giving norms of acting, enkindling efficacious fervor.

Matthew and Luke share a common point: the disciple they envisage is seen through members of the Church who perform certain charges and functions. This, however, does not prevent the two evangelists from reproducing the words of the historical Jesus. Exegesis has the task of making the necessary distinctions. Finally, Mark and Luke share a common point: an insistence on the disciple's lack of understanding. In Mark it is more generalized, while the secret of Luke bears particularly on the passion and death of Jesus. The disciple of the Lukan church finds in the fate of his Savior a force to withstand the test of time, and he must understand that his condition cannot be better than that of Jesus.

E. Jesus Communicates His Power to the Apostles

Because the gospel of Matthew is an ecclesiastical

book, it offers a particularly pointed reflection on the disciple's participation in the power and mission of Jesus. The great missionary discourse in chapter 10 is significant here. It presents an intended parallelism between Jesus and the disciples. God sends Jesus (Mt 10:40, 15:24); the disciples are sent (Mt 10:5). God gives *exousia*, divine power and authority, to Jesus, and Jesus gives *exousia* to his apostles (Mt 10:1). The work of the Messiah is expressed by *kerussein*, "to proclaim" (Mt 4:23, 9:35); the disciple does the same, his function is the same (Mt 10:7)—so much so that if we say that Jesus teaches and evangelizes, so does the disciple (Mt 11:5). Like Jesus, the disciple casts out demons (Mt 10:8). The disciples proclaim that the kingdom of heaven is at hand (Mt 10:7) because they are the salt of the earth and the light of the world. They must confine their activity to the cities of Israel (Mt 10:5-6, 15:24). They are prophets, like Jesus, and will receive similar treatment, including persecution (Mt 10:41, 5:12, 13:17, 23:34).

In the parables, Matthew glorifies the state of the disciples because of what their eyes have seen and their ears heard: "many a prophet and many a saint longed to see what you see but did not see it, to hear what you hear but did not hear it" (Mt 13:17). And once they have understood, Jesus tells them: "Every scribe who is learned in the reign of God is like the head of a household who can bring from his storeroom both the new and the old" (Mt 13:51-52).

F. *The Eschatological Dimension*

An essential aspect of the definition of disciple lies in the eschatological dimension of the preaching of the kingdom.

The expectation of the victory of God and his people over their enemies and the establishment of the pure

and perfect covenant which it brings gave rise, during
New Testament times, to an extraordinary religious
phenomenon which we must now take into account:
Qumran. This vast apocalyptic movement, of which
the book of Daniel is one of the most representative
witnesses, had already been marked by uneasiness and
preparation within certain Jewish circles with a view
to the coming end. The community of Qumran lived
and organized itself in the light of that expectation.
Its originality lay not only in its being set up in the
desert, in its "pre-monastic" structure, in its teaching
(both ascetic and mystical) in view of the desired perfection, but also in the radical demand it placed upon
its members. It was a sect which rejected official
Judaism and radicalized the precepts of the Torah
to such an extent that it added its own laws to the
Law of Moses. From its earliest settlement, as far as
we can reconstruct from the Community Rule manu-
script Qumran's piety was distinguished from Old
Testament piety by this excessive and small-minded
bent, which stands in dramatic contrast to the very
rich depths of its research into, and cult of, the Word
of God, as well as its total abnegation. From beginning
to end, the community kept alive an anxious expectation of the vengeful and saving act of the eschatological victory.

We find similar traits in the phenomenon of John
the Baptist. He is not a solitary; he makes disciples.
Nor is he only an ascetic with coarse clothes and
meager food. If he is in the desert, his activity is
inscribed by his proclamation of the decisive change
in the religious situation. Those who present themselves,
he baptizes—with a baptism beyond the Jewish rite
of purification. His baptism involves preparation and
entrance into the messianic and eschatological hope.
John's disciples are not at all like the students of the
rabbis. What distinguishes them from the disciples of
Jesus and the life and religious ideal of the new master.

John's disciples practice asceticism and fast (Mk 2:18); like him, they too eagerly look forward to "the day" (Lk 7:18-30; Mt 11:2-15); but they do not pretend that John is the Messiah. In fact, he himself forbade it (Mk 1:5-7). For this reason the radicalism which represents the depth of Jesus' message was missing in John's movement and disciples.

Because he declares that the prophetic expectation of the fullness of time is now fulfilled and that the kingdom of God is at hand, Jesus commits those who follow him to a perspective which, while not without shadows, determines their whole new life. The complete change of heart that is required supposes that one is well aware that the acts of the revealing and saving God acquire, with and through Jesus, a dimension unknown up till then, a dimension going beyond the Law and the prophets and abolishing the transitory norms of the established religion. Limitless perspectives are opened: "In a word, you must be made perfect as your heavenly Father is perfect" (Mt 5:48). The kingdom of God will come in power. In many statements the master unites the present time and the time when the end will come, as if we could expect this ultimate fulfillment soon. Since it shares in the totality of end-time realities, the present, in a way, becomes the end.

The present and the end-time interpenetrate so thoroughly that the personal situation of the disciple is determined not only by his hope and expectation but also by his present self-understanding. The disciple feels himself to be involved and committed in a great epic when he hears the master make such astonishing statements as these: "As to the exact day or hour, no one knows it, neither the angels in heaven, nor even the Son, but only the Father" (Mk 13:32; Mt 24:36); "I assure you, among those standing here there are some who will not taste death until they see the reign of God established in power" (Mk 9:1;

Mt 16:28; Lk 9:27); "I assure you, this generation will not pass away until all these things take place" (Mk 13:30); the Sanhedrin will see "The Son of Man seated at the right hand of the Power and coming with the clouds of heaven" (Mk 14:62).

The fate of the disciple also is well indicated: "If anyone in this faithless and corrupt age is ashamed of me and of my doctrine, the Son of Man will be ashamed of him when he comes with the holy angels in his Father's glory" (Mk 8:38; Mt 10:33; Lk 9:26, 12:8-9; Jn 8:51). Jesus, as witness or as judge, introduces the disciple into his own proper condition of glory where the feast of the elect will be celebrated (Mt 8:11-12; Lk 13:29). And as for the twelve, you "shall take your places on twelve thrones to judge the twelve tribes of Israel" (Q; Mt 1 9:28b; Lk 22:30).

This eschatological dimension does not only command hopeful expectation and vigilance, nor is it only the basis for a reward ethic; rather, it associates and unites the disciple and the master. The same definitive and eschatological act of God creates communion and sustains the radicalism of Jesus' demands. It makes of this communion with the master, accepted by the disciple's total faith, a common drama whose repercussions can scarcely be comprehended. Far from being diminished, expectation is increased as time goes on. The delay of the parousia is filtered back into the doctrines and words attributed to Jesus. The third gospel shows very clear traces of this development of thought. In order to preserve all the dynamism of the eschatological hope for nascent Christianity, the heads of the first communities had to vehemently attack the backslide into indifference.

G. Conclusion

If we try to group together these elements which we

have collected, the image of the disciple can be clearly perceived. Jesus enters into history with God's power and word, which radicalize this revealing and saving act. His person as well as his message constitute the gospel; he transcends the old Law and its interpreters; he tears down the hedges and removes the blinders of the communities so that the kingdom might bring about the conversion of souls and permit them to accept the fullness of time and the realization of the promised messianic age. He calls and chooses disciples with authority and separates them from the crowd, takes them into his entourage, groups them, instructs them. Those who are with him, adhering to his person and word by faith, are established in a new state of soul and of life; it is an interior attitude, a totally new condition. They live at the time when they must choose between salvation and damnation (Lk 4:18-21).

Sometimes Jesus addresses himself to all the disciples, emphasizing the action of the Father, which summons them—though they must follow Jesus—to an even greater love of neighbor. His life, his work, his word are revelations of a radical relationship between God and man and among men themselves. The attitude of the disciple toward material goods depends on that new word of God and on his participation in the community created by Jesus.

Along with this group of disciples, Jesus addressed himself in a special way to the most faithful, especially to the twelve. Here, among those who follow him to the end, is the concrete human situation where the transformation of the old economy is elaborated in its fullest form. This is the seed of the new people, called to absorb the old. For this small group especially, the presence of the master and the sight of his works of power permit a hope and an expectation which constitute powerful forces for unity and effectiveness. Further, Jesus and his followers enter into conflict with the

Jewish authorities because of his activity, which, the latter maintain, is exercised outside the bounds of their tradition. This lack of understanding and this rejection of his message isolate both the master and his disciples. Persecution contributes to uniting their lives and destinies.

This following of the gospel leads to living a community type of life, and it is in such a milieu that we must situate the messianic demands which characterize the call of Jesus.

II. The Demands

To believe the gospel and to follow Jesus: this means to obey the new commandments and to commit oneself to the way traced out by the master. It is not enough simply to listen, one must also do: "Why do you call me 'Lord, Lord,' and not put into practice what I teach you?" (Lk 6:46; Mt 7:21). The first gospel summed up this law of Jesus very well: "I tell you, unless your holiness surpasses that of the scribes and Pharisees you shall not enter the kingdom of God" (Mt 5:20). All the gospels report a saying which basically goes back to Jesus himself: "Whoever would preserve his life will lose it, but whoever loses his life for my sake and the gospel's will preserve it" (Mk 8:35; Lk 9:24, 17:33; Mt 16:25, 10:39; Jn 12:25). The true disciple is the laborer who declares, after his hard day's work, "We are useless servants. We have done no more than our duty" (Lk 17:10). If Jesus demands laborious and gratuitous acts, he nonetheless respects human freedom; he enlists only volunteers.

The radical nature of Jesus' demands appears in a series of statements that are rooted in two themes: (1) the kingdom of God and (2) mission. The words of Jesus belong to these two groups. In a first set of sayings, Jesus proclaims the conditions for all for entering into the kingdom. The second set is addressed to the disciples who are more closely united to Jesus. We will note that this radicalism is as much present in the first set as in the second.

A. *The Kingdom of God*

1. Entrance into God's kingdom is guarded by a narrow door, says Luke (13:24). To this Matthew adds (no doubt of his own composing) the rough road (7:13-1 4). Luke places the logion during the journey to Jerusalem, where Jesus teaches as he travels along. "Someone asked him," Luke adds, "Lord, are they few in number who are to be saved?" (13:23). This anonymous person, it seems, was not a disciple. Jesus answers in a more general way: "Try to come in through the narrow door" (Lk 13:24). Like Luke, Matthew has found the logion in Q, but has reworked it more than Luke by integrating it into the Sermon on the Mount (7:13-14). Here too it is a general instruction addressed to the disciples.

We can hardly accept the opinion that the narrow door alludes to martyrdom, the fate reserved for the disciples. Nor is it sufficient to read here only a moral or ascetic rule of severity in the conduct of the disciples. We cannot detach the saying from its messianic context: "Many, I tell you, will try to enter and be unable" (Lk 13:24). The kingdom—the narrow door—is not open to every passing breeze. Whoever wishes to enter must be aware of the severe demands. Let us keep the radicalism of the image.

2. Another saying of Jesus has a similar meaning: "Whoever puts his hand to the plow and keeps looking back is unfit for the reign of God" (Lk 9:62). This saying too, proper to Luke, was pronounced as the group surrounding Jesus was wending its way to Jeru-

salem. It is an anonymous disciple who declares,
"I will be your follower, Lord, but first let me take
leave of my people at home." Jesus responds with the
logion we have just cited.

The worker must use his whole strength if he is to
accomplish his task in a useful way with a very primitive tool. The earth must be turned over and the
furrows must not deviate from a straight line. The
plowman's attention is necessarily directed straight
ahead and he makes progress only through keeping
wholly, intensely alert. We clearly catch the image.
The kingdom of God is a field which requires total
commitment. The logion is thus at one with the first
demands, which we meet immediately before in the
same section (Lk 9:57-60).

3. Let us pass from this field imagery, which is not
without profundity, to a theme where the demand is
expressed in vigorous language.

> Some men are incapable of sexual activity from birth; some
> have been deliberately made so; and some there are who
> have freely renounced sex for the sake of God's reign. Let
> him accept this teaching who can (Mt 19:12).

Only Matthew reports this logion. Jesus has just had
a discussion with the Pharisees concerning divorce,
who seem to have left when "the disciples" say that
the prohibiton of divorcing one's wife is so harsh that
it is not expedient to mary. Jesus answers them, and
it is a difficult answer—but critics agree in not attributing it to Jesus. It is not genteel, and is very
difficult to use in catechetics or sermons, but we cannot deny that it expresses a call to the totality of
commitment. It reaches to the very depths of the one
who is called since it proposes to the disciples continence in and out of marriage.

Some have tried to avoid this conclusion and have
taken the words about the third category (those who

have freely renounced sex) as a historical statement of
Jesus. There were some, they say, such as the Essenes, who abstained from conjugal relations. Referring
then to the passage immediately preceding, which concludes "Not everyone can accept this teaching, only
those to whom it is given to do so" (19:11), they remove from verse 12 all of its striking force. An exegesis
like this remains totally isolated; there is nothing
here to make us thing that Jesus was speaking of
Essenes. In Judaism, castration is a dreadful thing, forbidden by the Law (Lev 22:24). If Jesus proposed this
to his disciples, he could have done so only symbolically. In the time of Jesus, to abstain from marriage was
viewed as a failure. Even the rabbis had a family.
We know of only one exception: Rabbi Ben Azzai,
who proclaims, "My soul is attached to the Torah;
the world is preserved for others" (Tos Job 8:4). His
colleagues did not forgive him this.

Jesus was not married and, he dared to break with
the ideas of his time because the kingdom assured the
gift of understanding and courage from God to those
who renounced women. If Jesus speaks of marriage in
a way which upset the disciples, he goes even further
and presents a mystery which begins a new relationship between the world and God. It is significant that
the passage ends with "Let him accept this teaching
who can" (Mt 19:12). The understanding of so unique
a call is of the same order as the prohibition of divorce: "Not everyone can accept this teaching, only
those to whom it is given to do so" (Mt 19:11). The
theocentrism of Matthew appears in all its force. God
alone can open our understanding and give strength
in the face of certain human renunciations. The gift
of God must be the base of the response of anyone
who makes himself a eunuch for the kingdom of God.

There is, however, a remarkable difference between
the two situations: the abolition of divorce is an ab-

solute precept, while vowing oneself to continence is presented as the ideal situation for those who wish to consecrate themselves radically to the kingdom.

4. We now enter an area where the call of Jesus cannot be subsumed under an image. In an anecdote reported by Mark (3:31-35), followed by the other synoptics (Mt 12:46-50; Lk 8:19-21; cf. Lk 11:7), the attitude of Jesus toward his mother and his relatives strikes us as rather strange: "Who are my mother and brothers. Whoever does the will of God is brother and sister and mother to me." Jesus has subordinated familial obligations to the service of the word of God, as Luke says, and, according to Mark and Matthew, to obedience to the new will of God to establish the kingdom. From this time on, it makes sense to demand of the totally committed disciple a clear attitude of freedom and of consecration to the new economy of salvation.

5. Jesus returns to this theme in two other logia, The first belongs to the Q source, where we find passages common to Matthew and Luke. Matthew inserts it in his great missionary discourse (10:37-38), where it is obviously part of a literary composition. Luke places it in his narrative of the Journey to Jerusalem. Since there are ample indications in tone and expression that Matthew's version is later, we will base our discussion on Luke's version. "On one occasion when a great crowd was with him, he turned to them and said . . . " This introduction, which tells us who Jesus' audience was, is typical Lukan redaction. Despite the presence of the crowd, the passage deals with an instruction destined for the disciples. The saying itself is of a different style: "If anyone comes to me without turning his back on (i.e., "hating") his father and mother, his wife and his children, his brothers and sisters, indeed his very self, he cannot be my follower" (Lk 14:25-26). Matthew re-

places "hate" with "to love more than"; he omits
"If anyone comes to me" which does not fit his context, the missionary discourse; he twice writes "is not
worthy of me," which is typical of his theology. Likewise, Matthew's "son or daughter" becomes Luke's
"his children." Luke also completes Matthews list with
"and his wife and his sisters, indeed his very self."
Lk 14:26-27 and Mt 10:37 were used in the gospel of
Thomas and had a great influence in the early church.
Clement of Alexandria and Epiphanius refer to them
explicitly.

Jesus did not bind a person to familial obligations.
The logion was inspired by Micah (7:6), which proclaims the division of families which would follow the
descent of fire on the earth, the coming of the kingdom. In the view of Luke, "wife," "sisters," and
"self" expand the logion with an even more pronounced radicalism.

6. The second passage, appearing in the triple tradition, is no less significant (Mk 28-31; Mt 19:27-30;
Lk 18:28-30). These texts present many literary problems which we cannot deal with here, but the three
gospels agree in connecting the proclamation of Jesus
to a statement of Peter. In Mark and Matthew
(19:27 a-b), Peter affirms: "Here we have put everything aside to follow you." "Put everything aside"
becomes in Luke "we have let all we own." Is this
a real remembrance or a literary precision? Or is it
a primitive formula in a form less traditional and
less influenced by the responses in the "vocation call"
forms?

In any case, the three evangelists have Jesus begin
his response with "I solemnly assure you (Amen)."
This formula, which Luke takes up here (contrary to
his usual practice), introduces a prophetic oracle and
is equivalent to "Thus says Yahweh" (or the agent of
his revelation). In the name of this supreme authority,

the reward in this life and in eternal life is assured to him who has left house (the three plurals in Mt) or wife (only Lk) or brothers (all three) or sisters (Mk and Mt) or father (Mk and Mt) for the sake of my name (Mt), for the sake of me and of the gospel (Mk), for the sake of the kingdom of God (Lk), who will surely receive a hundred times as much (Mk), will receive many times as much and inherit . . . (Mt) a plentiful return(Lk).

In mentioning the possessions and activities to be left behind, Luke pursues his problematic on effective poverty. He remains consistent with himself in naming "wife" among the things to be left behind. Again we see in Luke an intentional emphasis and a more pronounced radicalism. Would he have added "wife", he who is so favorable to women, if his source had not contained it?

7. Another "family" logion is most expressive for our purpose. "Another, a disciple, said to him, "Lord, let me go and bury my father first." But Jesus told him, 'Follow me, and let the dead bury their dead' " (Mt 8:21-22). Luke's version of the saying is secondary (Lk 9:60), but a common origin is certain; it is a very ancient tradition. Matthew and Luke place the saying in the context of the following of Jesus. Matthew presents two cases, while Luke has three. We have already discussed the first case of Matthew and Luke (foxes have dens) and the third case of Luke (the hand set to the plow). It is impossible to fix with certitude the place and time when Jesus pronounced this logion.

The meaning of Jesus' response cannot be watered down. We weaken it if we say that Jesus demands the disciples' continual presence near himself and commands then to set the matters of the kingdom ahead of those of the family. We distort its meaning when we say that the father, a very old man, has died and that the son must not make a trip which would benefit no one. The vital dimension of the paradigm is much more paradoxical because Jesus receives the order of human values and their legitimate concerns. If we belong to Jesus' following, we must be totally subject to the master and aware of the radicalism of this new economy of salvation, which can set us against "good sense" and the most legitimate demands of filial piety. It would, again, devalue Jesus' saying were we to understand "the dead" in the sense of spiritual death, even though the word *nekros* can have an allegorical meaning at times.

To refuse a disciple the right to go and bury his father formally contradicts Jewish law and customs. In Judaism, the fourth commandment covered this duty of piety. To bury one's father dispensed one from all the commandments of the Torah, even from study of the Torah itself. In such an instance, one does not contract legal impurity, whereas the touching of a cadaver would render both the high priest and the Nazirite impure. We possess many ancient accounts in which a son leaves all to go and bury his father. This injunction of Jesus belongs with Matthew's antitheses: "As for me, I say to you . . ." In fact, this command could be set against the precept of charity so often emphasized by the master.

The one who is called finds himself committed to a new kind of religious experience to the point that the demands and the totality of this tie enjoin him to oppose other values. He is united to the career and the person of Jesus, and this takes precedence over the most fundamental religious and human obligations.

B. *Mission and Earthly Goods*

The narrow gate, the hand on the plow, the eunuch, the new family founded on God's word, hatred of

144

one's family, the leaving of every material and familial attachment, even to not burying one's father—these clearly show us the radicalism of Jesus in his preaching of the kingdom. Shortly we will pose the problem of whether such a program could actually be accomplished; here we will present the radicalism Jesus demands of those he sends out on mission.

1. Let us begin by recalling that Jesus was a poor man. However, nothing indicates that his family lived in misery. The carpenter of Nazareth earned his living with his hands; in his public life, he was never accused of doing it for gain. He could proclaim that he had nowhere to lay his head. Friendly houses received him; the apostolic group lived from the largesse of the women who accompanied it. An apostle, the traitor Judas, had charge of the common purse. The respect and enthusiasm which Jesus' preaching aroused opened the doors even of the rich, and Jesus did not refuse their hospitality. [6] His sayings on abandoning ourselves to providence and on the certainity of help from the Father would have had little meaning if Jesus, in his daily life, had been preoccupied with the cares of this world. No matter how critical one may be of the gospel texts, this image of Jesus regarding the goods of this world seems to be well founded.

"The poor you will always have with you" (Mk 14:7), declares Jesus. He lived very close to manual laborers: the cultivator of the field (Mk 4:3; Lk 9:62), laborers in the vineyard (Mt 20:1-15), the fisherman on the lake (Mt 13:47-50), the woman working in the house (Mt 13:33 and parallels), servants and domestic slaves (Lk 12:36-38, 17:7-10), and around him moved artisans and merchants, bricklayers, laborers, publicans, soldiers, kings and ministers, judges and doctors, property owners and stewards, country people and city folk. In Israel, manual labor was not looked down upon, as in other civilizations of the time.

2. Two preliminary remarks must be grasped in order to understand Jesus' demands of those whom he sent on mission. On the one hand, as R. Schnackenburg says, "we must leave the sayings of Jesus their hardness and their roughness." On the other, must we limit these radical demands on the disciple and his mission to the time of Jesus? It seems we cannot do this. Jesus' message founded an economy of salvation, a new people, whose witnesses and authorized preachers desired to fully realize the will of the master.

From the time the pastoral community was formed, we see the need for teaching. Without giving up expectation of the definitive coming of the kingdom, the church of Jerusalem began to expand, first gaining Syria and then all the known world. When the gospel tradition was formed, the expansion had progressed into the Hellenistic world, if not to Rome itself. Around A.D. 70, when the synoptic redactions began, we are in the time of the written book: for Luke, a glance back over the glorious past; for Matthew, a writing down of Jesus' oral catechesis. There is evolution but no discontinuity. The preaching of the kingdom and the conditions for the mission's success necessitate recourse to traditions as old as possible. The time of Jesus' preaching becomes the special time from which one seeks out the demands and the norms for the present.

Thus the purpose of the gospels is to fix the rules of the various communities by making them participate in the happenings before Easter and, by addding to these words and happenings in the ecclesial coloring, which is indeed the seal of their continuity. The canonization of the books carried the canonization of the words and actions of Jesus a further step.

From the social point of view, the disciples of Jesus led the same life as their master. Moreover, those who were called to the kingdom must become "fishers of men" (Mk 1:7) and harvesters of God (Lk 10:2).

We have just pointed out the radical demands within the context of being sent on mission. If we treat in more detail the sayings of Matthew and Luke on what the missionary should take with him, we fear we will repeat what Fathers Dupont and Légasse have so well explained. However, we cannot avoid this completely. Particular instructions are given those who went on mission, and Luke and Matthew have synthesized them clearly.

3. Luke has integrated into the teaching of chapter 14 the conditions for the missionary disciple, who renounce everything he holds dear. This demand is repeated twice—placed a bit arbitrarily (in one verse) at the end of two parables. In this way Luke teaches the prudence that is required to commit oneself completely: he must know that ''in the same way, none of you can be my disciple if he does not renounce all his possessions'' (Lk 14:33; cf. 12:33). In the same context, Luke places the breaking of family ties and the carrying of the cross (14:25-27). In addition, we have, in the same journey narrative, two Lukan groupings in which freedom regarding the goods of the world is the condition for being a missionary. In chapter 12 he prescribes trusting oneself to providence and not amassing treasure, selling one's goods, and giving alms (12:13-34). Similar logia are brought together in chapter 16 (16:9, 10-12).

In these small, Lukan syntheses we become aware that the question of material things was more and more preoccupying the church of Luke and that, far from concealing the words of Jesus on this subject, he comes back to them, giving them their realistic application. In chapter 10, where Luke has sent seventy-two disciples on mission, the two themes of the equipment of the missionary and his life of poverty during his mission are tied together. Luke takes these precepts from the triple tradition (Lk 10:4-12; Mt 10:9-16) or has recourse to doublets (9:3-5, 42, 10:4-16).

Matthew organized his great synthesis in the missionary discourse of chapter 10, the so-called missionary's breviary. A double perspective dominates the writing: the time of Jesus and the time of the Church; and it is quite difficult to precisely delineate their fields of application.

4. These Lukan and Matthean groupings of the demands on the missionary brings this double perspective together to underline the radical demands of Jesus as applied to the situation of the apostolic Church. The way Luke and Matthew develop the teaching to actualize Jesus' message for the Church of their time bears consequences for the religious life of the primitive Church. The message of Jesus is valid for the Church for all time. The community finds its vital thrust and purification by constantly referring to the calls which manifest the eschatological will of God in Jesus. It does not deny the radical statements: "Whoever breaks the least significant of these commands and teaches others to do so shall be called least in the kingdom of God. Whoever fulfills and teaches these commands shall be great in the kingdom of God" (Mt 5:19).

To those who object that the demands of Jesus are humanly impossible, the Church replies with another saying of the master, "For man it is impossible, but not for God. With God all things are possible" (Mk 10:26-27). The renunciation of earthly goods is part of this eschatology. The end-time is not just a motif, it creates a state of mind and gives a just appreciation of the new values. Moreover, even at the level of the texts and the life of the primitive Church, the radicalism of the demands concerning the abandonment of goods is not a precept to be put on the same footing as *metanoia* (conversion) and charity. It is part of a radicalism, a call to a total belonging to the kingdom and the person of the master, that is reserved to voluntary commitment. It would be too much to say that Jesus wished a double morality, one of precepts and one of counsels; but the calls of Jesus, interpreted by the synoptics, contain the germ of these later ecclesiastical developments. Their interpretation in a radical sense cannot appear simply as a human creation reaching out to meet the divine revelation.

Conclusion

I would like to sketch a last theme (disguised as a conclusion) which is not directly in line with those we have already met. We have developed the radical condition of the disciple in the light of the *sequela Christi*. The exemplarity and the imitation of Christ are clearly taught in a very important passage. After the Last Supper, Luke has placed an episode in which the disciples argue among themselves over who would be the greatest. Jesus says to them that they must not insist, as kings do, on the title "benefactor": "Let the greater among you be as the junior, the leader as the servant." He who is at the table is greater than he who serves. And then the statement of the master falls like a knife: "I am in your midst as the one who serves you" (Lk 22:24-27).

This saying is not only an affirmation of the humility of Jesus but is the basis of the disciples' imitation of him. This theme will be taken up again, and enlarged and deepened by the theologies of Paul and John. For the former it leads to incorporation into the mystical body; for the latter, to that unity between the disciple and the Son that is analogous to the way in which the Father and the Son are one. And in this way the vocation of the disciple to consecration and holiness is clarified. It is the logical consequence of what the historical Jesus had said and done.

This prolongation into the apostolic Church, once

made would lead the great Church toward later developments. The radicalism of the word and teaching of the synoptics has given the Christian movement the interior dynamism which molds the souls of those who, seeking God, receive from his love the strength to reply to the call of Jesus, to respond to it literally. At times, as with St. Francis in his two rules, this can take the form of the organization of an Order. The *vita apostolica* was transformed into monastic observance, and the itinerant ideal of the apostles became the imitation of Jesus and the apostles.

(THE END)

Footnotes

1. See our remarks at the end of the translator's preface regarding the footnotes for this chapter. Here we would just mention several of the works frequently cited by Fr. Rigaux: G. Bornkamm, *Jesus of Nazareth* (New York: Harper & Row, 1960); M. Hengel, *Nachfolge und Charisma* (Berlin: A. Topelmann, 1968); E. Lohse, "Nachfolge Christi," *RGG*, pp. 1286-1288; K. H. Schelke, *Discipleship and Priesthood* (New York: Herder & Herder, 1965); R. Schnackenburg, *The Moral Teaching of the New Testament* (New York: Herder & Herder, 1965); A. Schulz, *Nachfolge und Nachahmen* (Munich: V. Kosel, 1962).

2. Mk 1:17, 20, 8:34, Mt 4:19, 10:38, 16:24; Lk 9:23, 14:27. This terminology does not appear in Paul or John. *Akoloutheō* ("accompany") can be applied to the crowd but is used much more often of disciples: Mk 1:18, 20, 2:14, 6:1, 8:34 (twice), 10:21, 28, etc. Luke, Matthew, and John used the expression, but it occurs only once in Paul (1 Cor 10:4), where he is dependent on the Old Testament.

3. Mk 1:17, 20, 8:34; Mt 4:19, 10:38, 16:24; Lk 9:23, 14:27 (*deute*); *ekalēsen*: Mk 1:20; Mt. 4:21; *akolouthei*: Mk 2:14; 1:18, 6:1, etc.; Lk 5:11, 27, 28, etc.; *anedeixen:* Lk 10:1, Acts 1:24 (only occurrences in the New Testament).

4. Mk 2:15, 3:9, 5:31, 6:45, 8:34, 9:14, 10:46.

5. Mk 2:19, 3:7, 14, 4:36, 5:18, 40, 8:10, 9:28, 11:11, 14:14, 17, 18, 20, 33.

6. Mt 8:20; Lk 9:58. On the women accompanying Jesus, sees Lk 23:49; Jn 12:6 and 13:29 mention the common purse. On Jesus' receiving the friendship and hospitality of those who are well off, see Lk 7:36, 14:1. Enemies reproach him with being a glutton and a drunkard (Mt 11:19; Lk 7:34). Among his friends were Nicodemus (Jn 3:1-21), Joseph of Arimathea (Jn 19:38-39), and the rich Zaccahaeus (Lk 19:1-10).